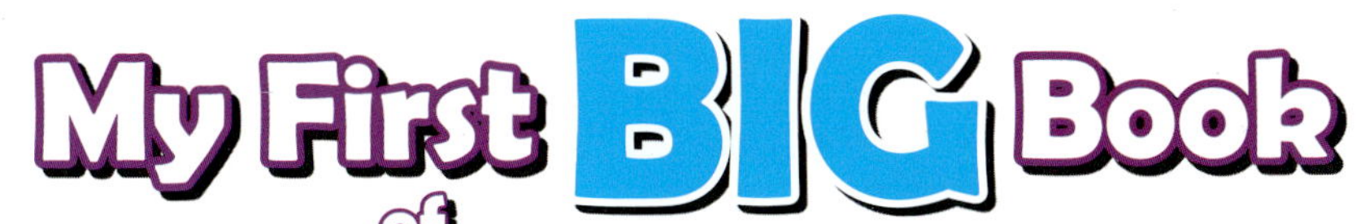

My First BIG Book of WHALES AND DOLPHINS

by Belinda Gallagher

Ruby Tuesday Books

Published in 2026 by Ruby Tuesday Books Ltd.

Copyright © 2026 Ruby Tuesday Books Ltd.

All rights reserved. No part of this publication may be reproduced in whole or in part, stored in any retrieval system, or transmitted in any form or by any means, electronic, mechanical, photocopying, recording, or otherwise, without written permission from the publisher.

Editors: Ruth Owen & Mark J. Sachner
Design & Production: Emma Randall

Photo credits: Alamy: 39B (imageBROKER.com), 47T (Arterra Picture Library), 49B (Joe Blossom), 54T (All Canada Photos), 55 (Chris Mattison), 61T (Bert de Ruiter), 63T (WILDLIFE GmbH), 71B (Brandon Cole Marine Photography), 76 (Derek Mitchell); Stefan Christmann (Nature Picture Library): 40–41, 42; Corbis: 17B; Katherine Feng (Nature Picture Library): 16B, 18; FLPA: 36T, 39T, 46, 48B, 49T; Getty Images: 37T; Eric Isselee (Shutterstock): 4B, 5T, 12T, 26T, 93B; iStock: 33T (wwing); Macrovector (Shutterstock): 91, 92T; Nature Picture Library: 7B (Ingo Arndt), 14T (Nick Upton), 14B (Jose Luis Alamy: 4, 12 (Waterframe), 8T, 36 (Andrey Nekrasov), 37B (NOAA), 56T (Juniors Bildarchiv GmbH), 59B (Steven J. Kazlowski), 63 (Wildestanimal), 69T (Minden Pictures), 69C (All Canada Photos), 78T (Toni Massot), 79T (Whittaker Wildlife UK), 80 (Anthony Pierce), 89C (D. Romeo/VW Pics); Simon Allen: 39B; Blue Planet Archive LLC (Alamy): 17T, 47, 72; Mark Carwardine (NPL): 9T, 11B, 66B, 73B; dpa picture alliance (Alamy): 11T, 22T, 25B, 29T; istock Photo: 71; James Kuether: 23; Nature Picture Library (NPL): Cover C (Klein & Hubert), 5B (Solvin Zankl), 13C (Doc White), 17B (Terry Whittaker), 27 (Pascal Kobeh), 41T (Franco Banfi), 44T (Conrad Maufe), 49 (Kathryn Jeffs), 58T (Martha Holmes), 60B (Shane Gross), 64–65 (Alex Mustard), 67T, 91T (Chase Dekker), 67B (Hiroya Minakuchi), 69B (Bertie Gregory), 77B (Kevin Schafer), 83T (Chris & Monique Fallows), 85T (Tony Wu), 86B (Brandon Cole); Flip Nicklin (NPL): 6T, 55B, 65T, 65B, 79B; NOAA: 87B; Saucoin (Creative Commons): 52; Science Photo Library: 18T (Roman Uchytel), 18B, 46B (Mikkel Juul Jenson), 43 (Claus Lunau), 45B (Sinclair Stammers); Shutterstock: Cover TL (Graig Lambert Photography), cover BR (slowmotiongli), 5T, 6B, 7, 8B, 9B, 10, 13T, 13B, 14, 15T, 16, 17C, 19–20, 24, 25T, 26, 28B, 29B, 30–31, 32–33, 34–35, 38, 39T, 40T, 41B, 42, 44B, 46T, 48, 50–51, 53, 56B, 57, 58B, 59T, 61–62, 66T, 68, 70, 74–75, 76, 77T, 78B, 81, 82, 84, 85B, 86, 87T, 88, 89T, 89B, 90, 91B, 92–93 (for a detailed contributor list contact: info@rubytuesdaybooks.com); Brian Skerry (NPL): 40B, 55T, 83B; Superstock: 15B, 28T (Michael Nolan), 18C (Nobumichi Tamura), 21 (Lex van Groningen), 45T (Franco Banfi), 54 (Corey Ford), 60T (alimdi/Arterra).

Library of Congress Control Number: 2025946369

Print (Hardback) ISBN 978-1-78856-633-9
Print (Paperback) ISBN 978-1-78856-634-6
ePub ISBN 978-1-78856-635-3

Published in Minneapolis, MN
Printed in the United States

www.rubytuesdaybooks.com

What's Inside?

What Are Whales and Dolphins?

Whales and dolphins are mammals that live in the ocean.

They breathe air and are **warm-blooded**.

Whales and dolphins give birth to babies that drink milk from their moms.

There's another animal that's a relative of whales and dolphins.

It's called a porpoise.

Are Dolphins a Type of Whale?

Yes! Dolphins are actually small toothed whales.

They live in family groups and hunt for food as a team.

Dolphins have beak-like snouts.

These playful bottlenose dolphins are taking turns leaping out of the water as they swim.

Porpoises are also small toothed whales. They live alone or in small groups.

The biggest type of dolphin is the orca.

How Many Types of Whales, Dolphins, and Porpoises Are There?

There are more than 90 different types! They are sorted into two main groups.

Toothed Whales

Toothed whales, including dolphins and porpoises, have rows of teeth for grabbing **prey**.

A toothed whale has one **blowhole** on top of its head for breathing.

Baleen Whales

These whales have sieve-like parts called **baleen plates** inside their mouths.

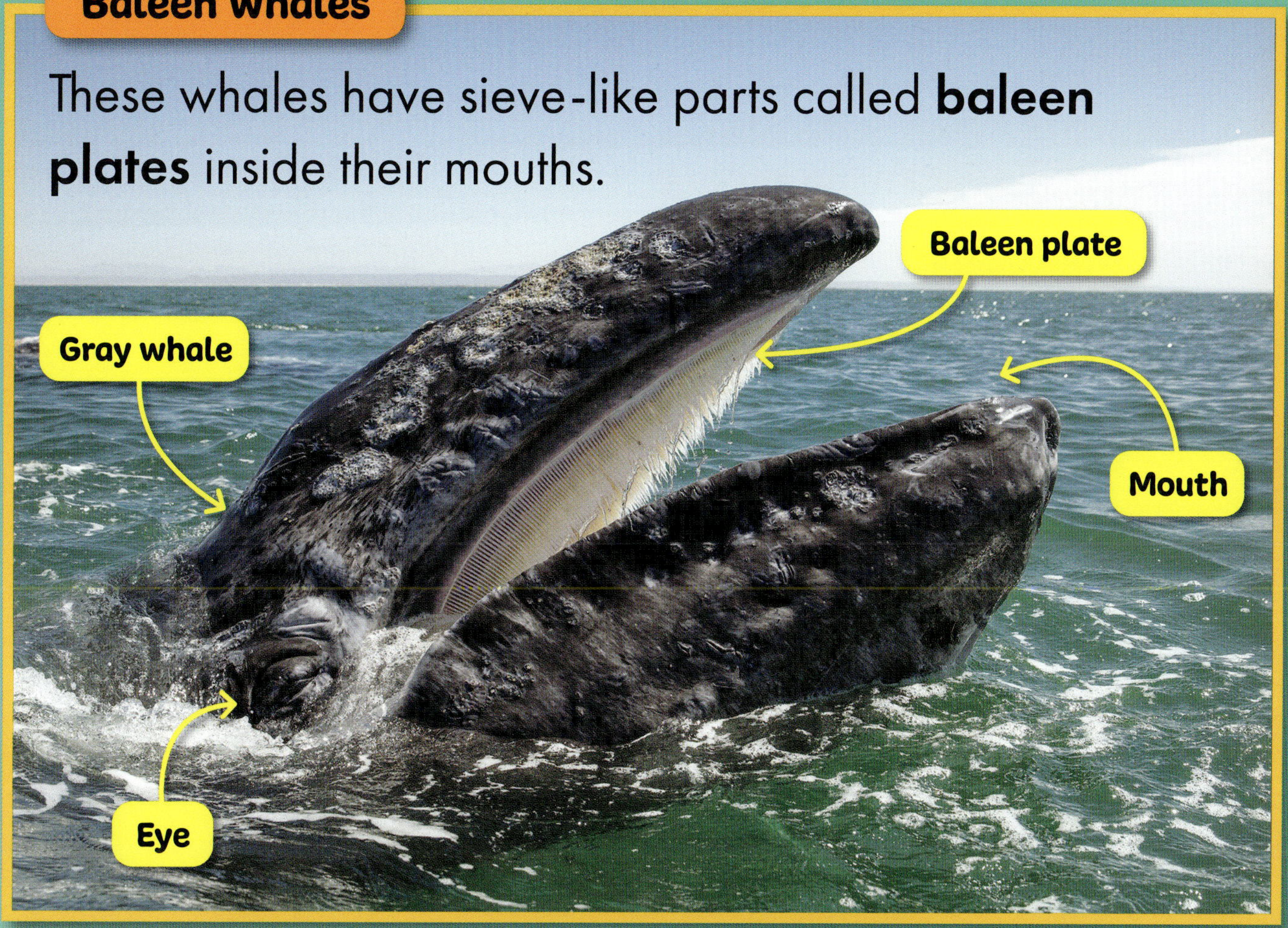

Baleen plate
Gray whale
Mouth
Eye

The whales gulp giant mouthfuls of water.

Then the baleen plates trap tiny animals that are in the water.

A baleen whale has two blowholes for breathing.

Are All Whales Big?

Yes! All whales are big animals. But some are super-size giants.

Blue whale 100 feet (30 meters) long

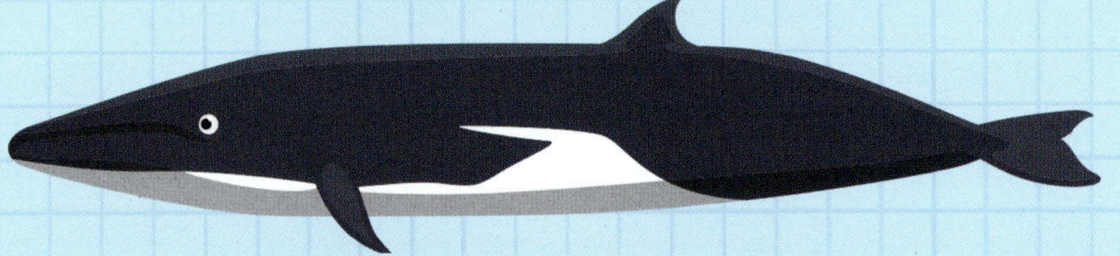

Fin whale 85 ft (26 m) long

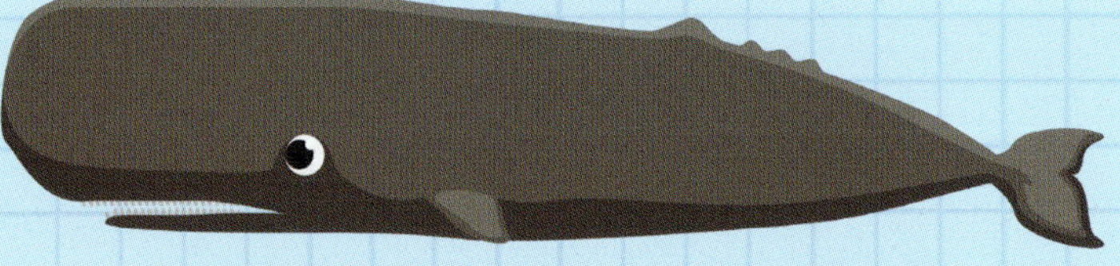

Sperm whale 65 ft (20 m) long

Bowhead whale 60 ft (18 m) long

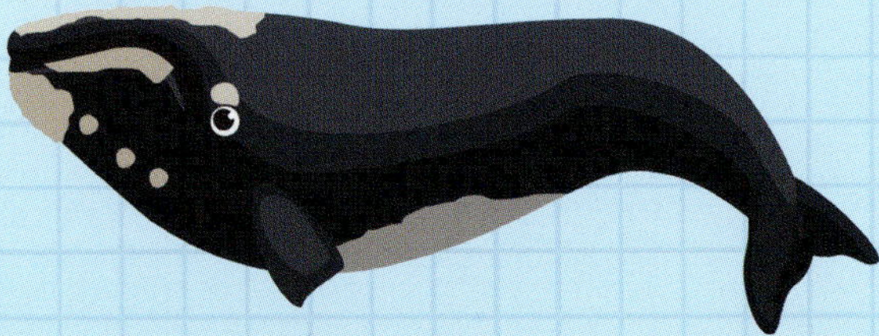

Right whale 55 ft (17 m) long

Look at these five ENORMOUS whales.

A blue whale has the biggest heart on Earth!

It pumps more than 9,000 pints (5,000 liters) of blood around the whale's huge body.

A model of a blue whale's heart

The mighty fin whale is the second-biggest whale.

A fin whale feeding

This fast swimmer moves at 30 miles per hour (48 km/h).

Who Is the Biggest of All?

The blue whale is the biggest animal to have ever lived on Earth.

It's even bigger than the biggest dinosaur!

Blue whale

A blue whale's eyes look tiny.

But they are still as big as grapefruits!

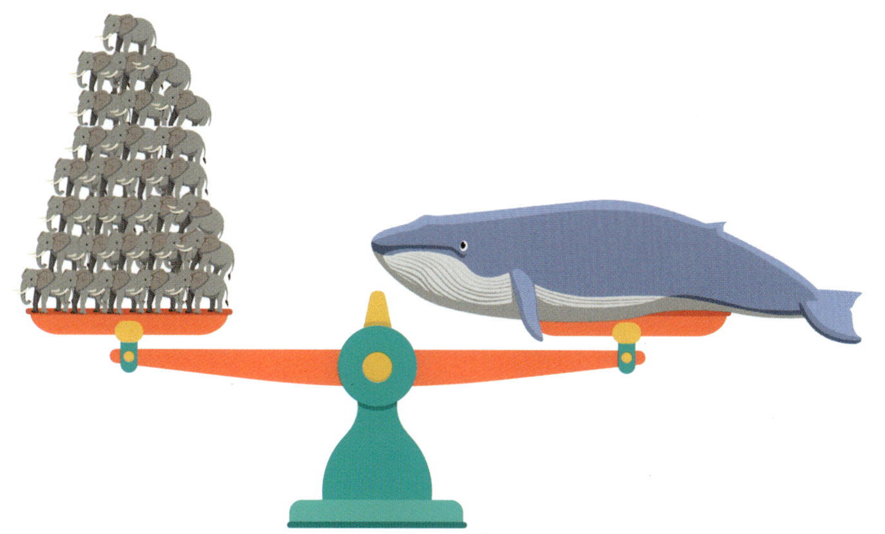

A blue whale weighs the same as 30 elephants!

The whale's mouth is so big, it can gulp its body weight in water.

A krill

Scientist's finger

A blue whale feeds on tiny, shrimp-like animals called krill.

A blue whale eats tons of tiny krill every day—it adds up to the weight of three elephants!

Who Makes the Biggest Splash?

Sometimes whales and dolphins leap out of the water and land with a splash. This is called breaching.

The biggest splash belongs to the humpback whale!

Whales also slap their tails on the water. This is called lobtailing.

This may be a way to show other whales who will be the best mate.

Spinner dolphin

Spinner dolphins may spin up to seven times as they breach!

Who Loves to Play Games?

Play is important for dolphins. They chase, leap, and have fun in the waves.

Being playful keeps dolphin family groups close to each other.

Dolphins also love to surf on big waves—just like human surfers!

Dolphins have been seen carrying pufferfish in their mouths—and passing them to each other.

Pufferfish

Pufferfish

Are the dolphins playing a fun pufferfish ball game?

They've also been spotted carrying octopuses and sea cucumbers.

They even play with seaweed at the water's surface.

Did Whales Once Live on Land?

Yes! The long-ago relatives of whales were land mammals with four legs.

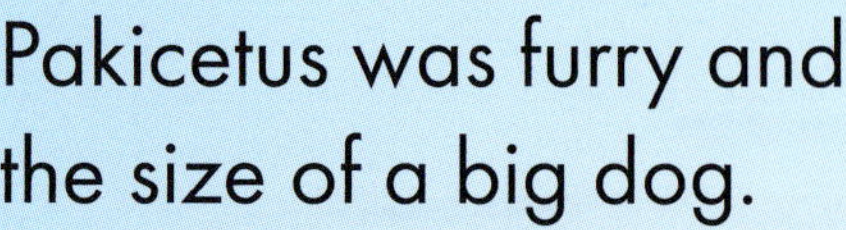

Pakicetus was furry and the size of a big dog.

It lived 50 million years ago.

Ambulocetus

Ambulocetus had webbed feet for swimming. But it could still use its legs to walk on land.

It lived 47 million years ago.

Dorudon

Dorudon spent all its life in water.

Flipper

It lived 40 million years ago.

Over millions of years, these animals changed into water mammals with **flippers** instead of legs.

These **skeletons** show how the **prehistoric** animals slowly changed to become whales.

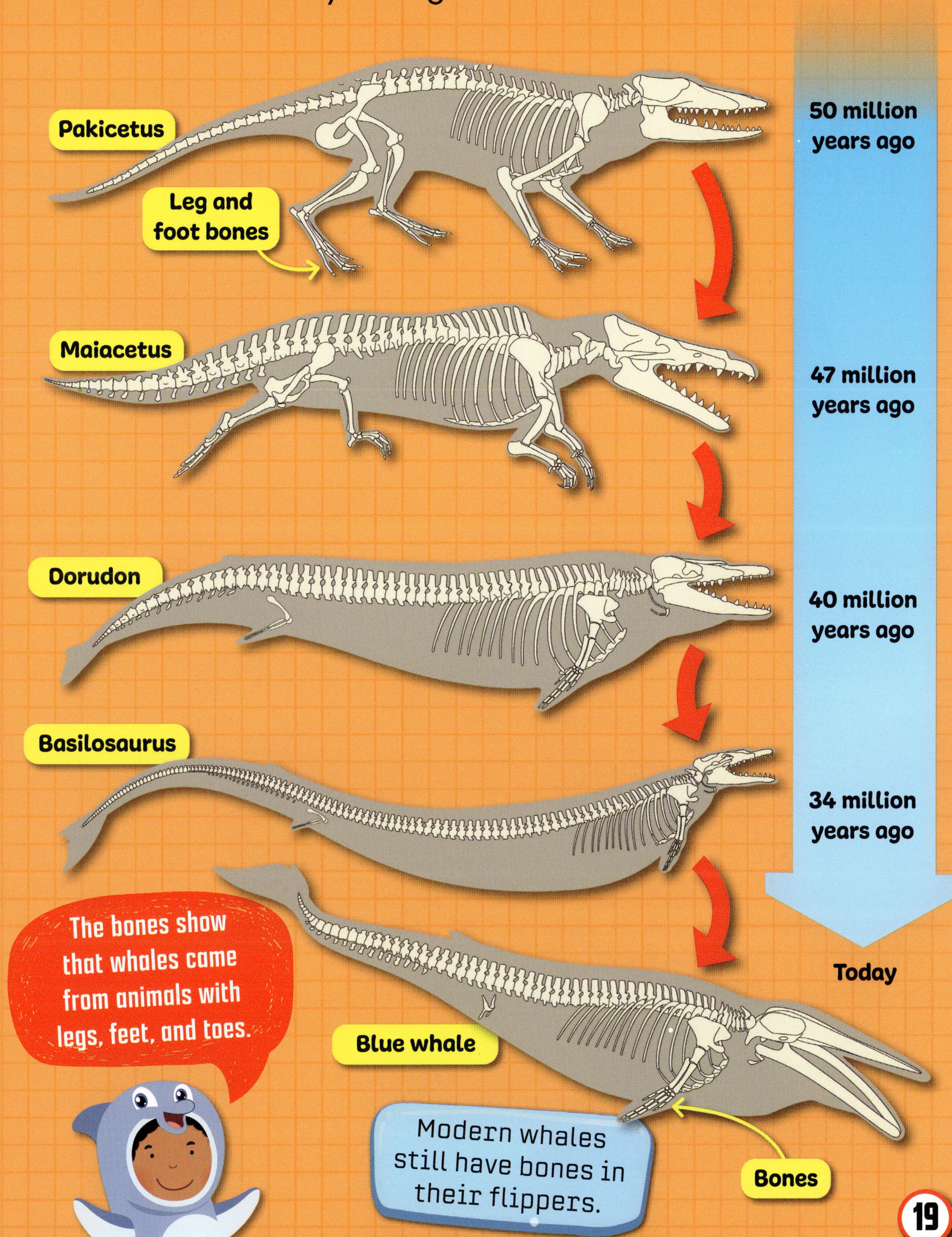

Which Whale Had the Biggest Teeth of All Time?

Livyatan was a huge prehistoric whale.

It lived about 12 million years ago.

Livyatan was a fierce hunter of big animals such as sharks and other whales.

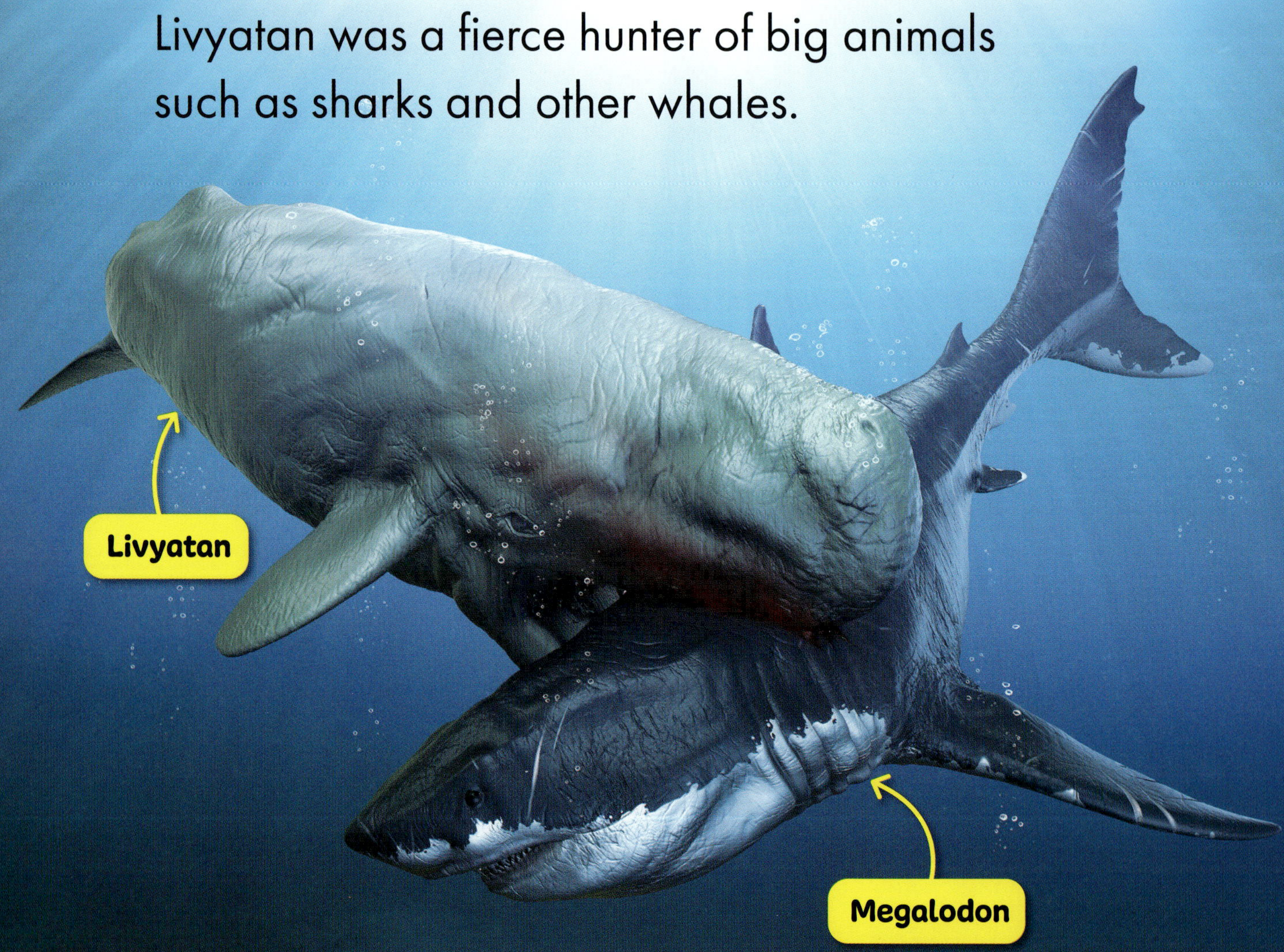

It shared its ocean home with Megalodon—the biggest shark of all time!

Livyatan was a prehistoric relative of sperm whales.

This is a **fossil** of its giant head and mouth.

Livyatan had the biggest teeth of any hunting animal that ever lived.

Which Prehistoric Whale Was a Monster?

It was Perucetus—a monster-sized whale! It lived about 40 million years ago.

A scientist discovered some fossil bones of this whale in 2010.

The fossil bones are super-thick and heavy.

The fossils were found in a desert in Peru. The desert was once a prehistoric ocean.

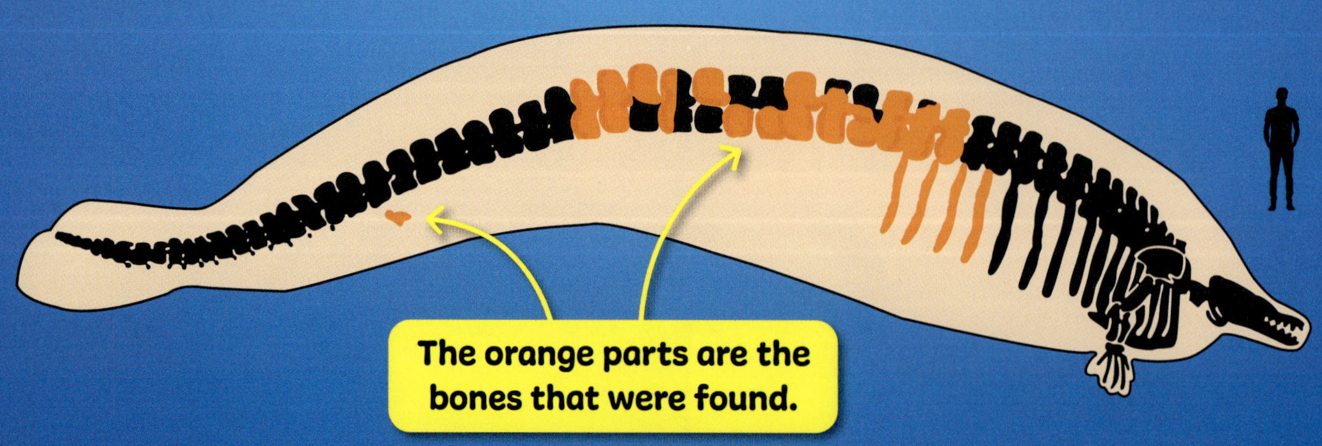

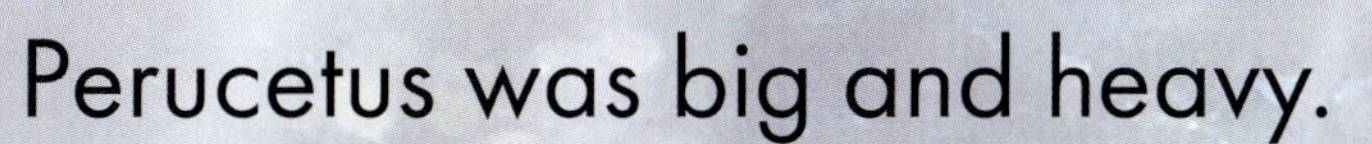

Perucetus was big and heavy.

It was probably a slow swimmer that lived in shallow water.

Perucetus

Perucetus may have eaten foods such as shellfish and crabs.

This whale possibly weighed more than 10 elephants!

What's Inside Whales and Dolphins?

Like all mammals, whales and dolphins have muscles and a skeleton made of bones.

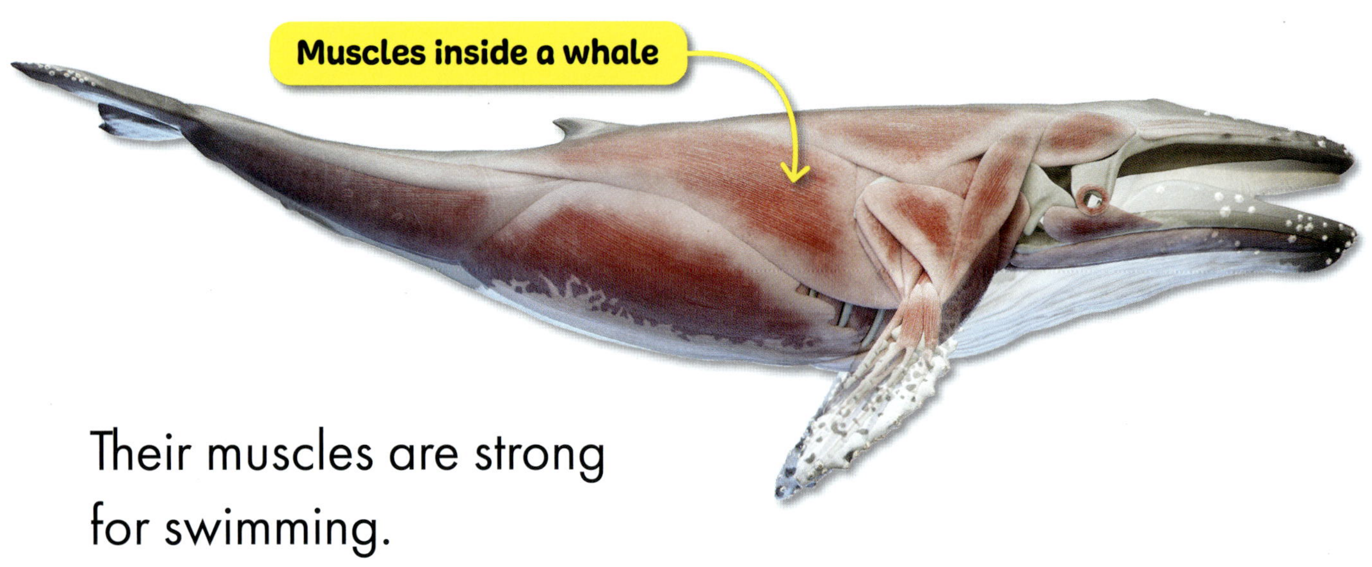

Their muscles are strong for swimming.

They have lightweight bones to help them float.

Whales and dolphins have body parts such as lungs, a heart, intestines, and a brain.

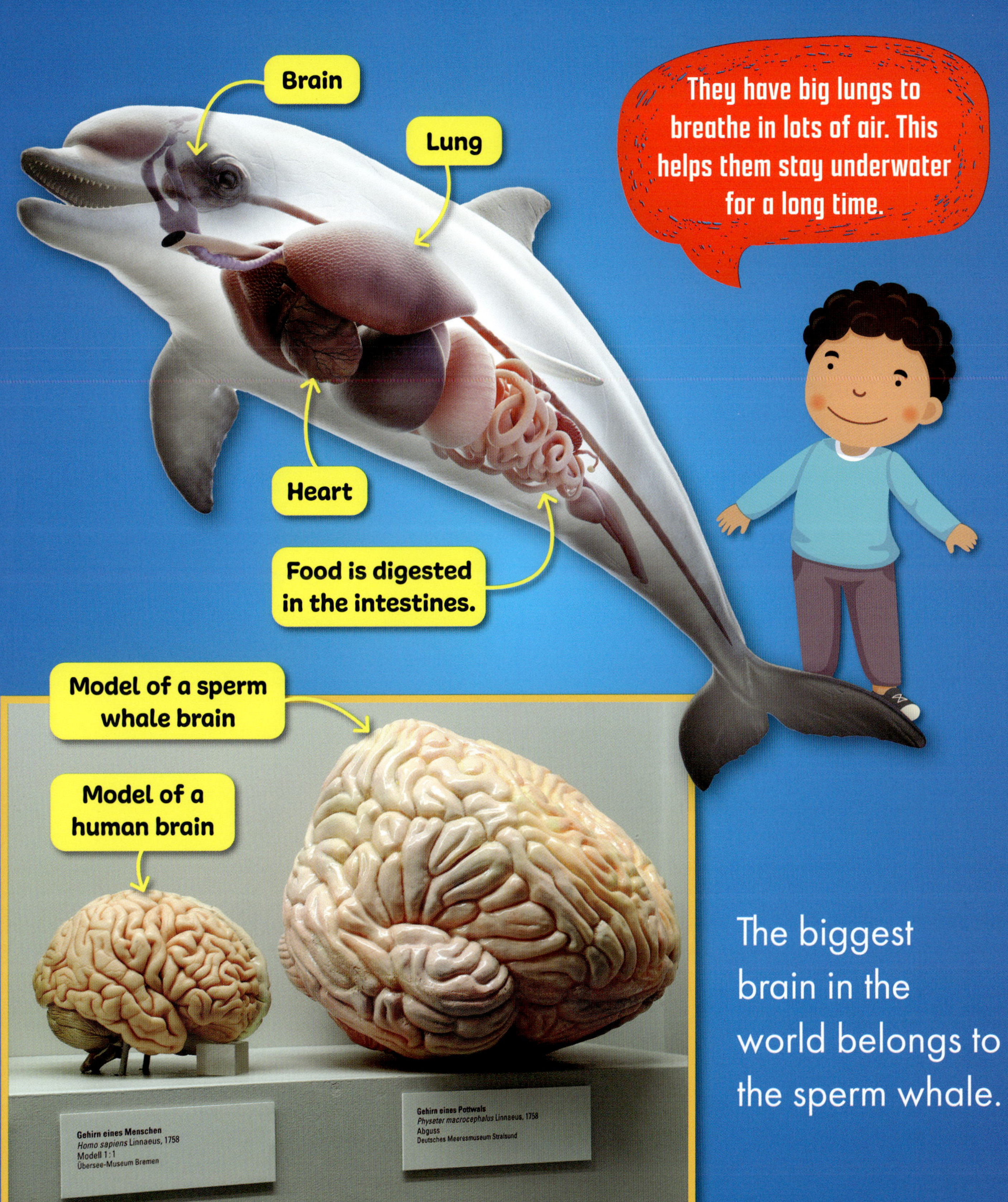

The biggest brain in the world belongs to the sperm whale.

How Do Whales and Dolphins Swim?

Whales and dolphins use their tails and two front flippers to swim.

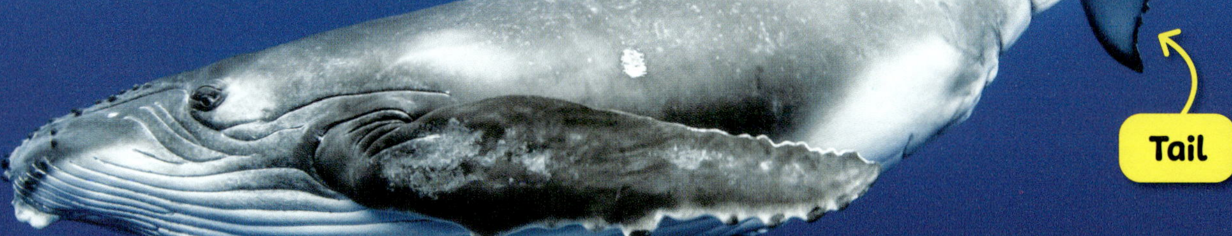

A smooth, **streamlined** body moves easily through water.

A whale, dolphin, or porpoise's tail is called a **fluke**.

A sperm whale's fluke

It moves up and down and pushes the animal forward.

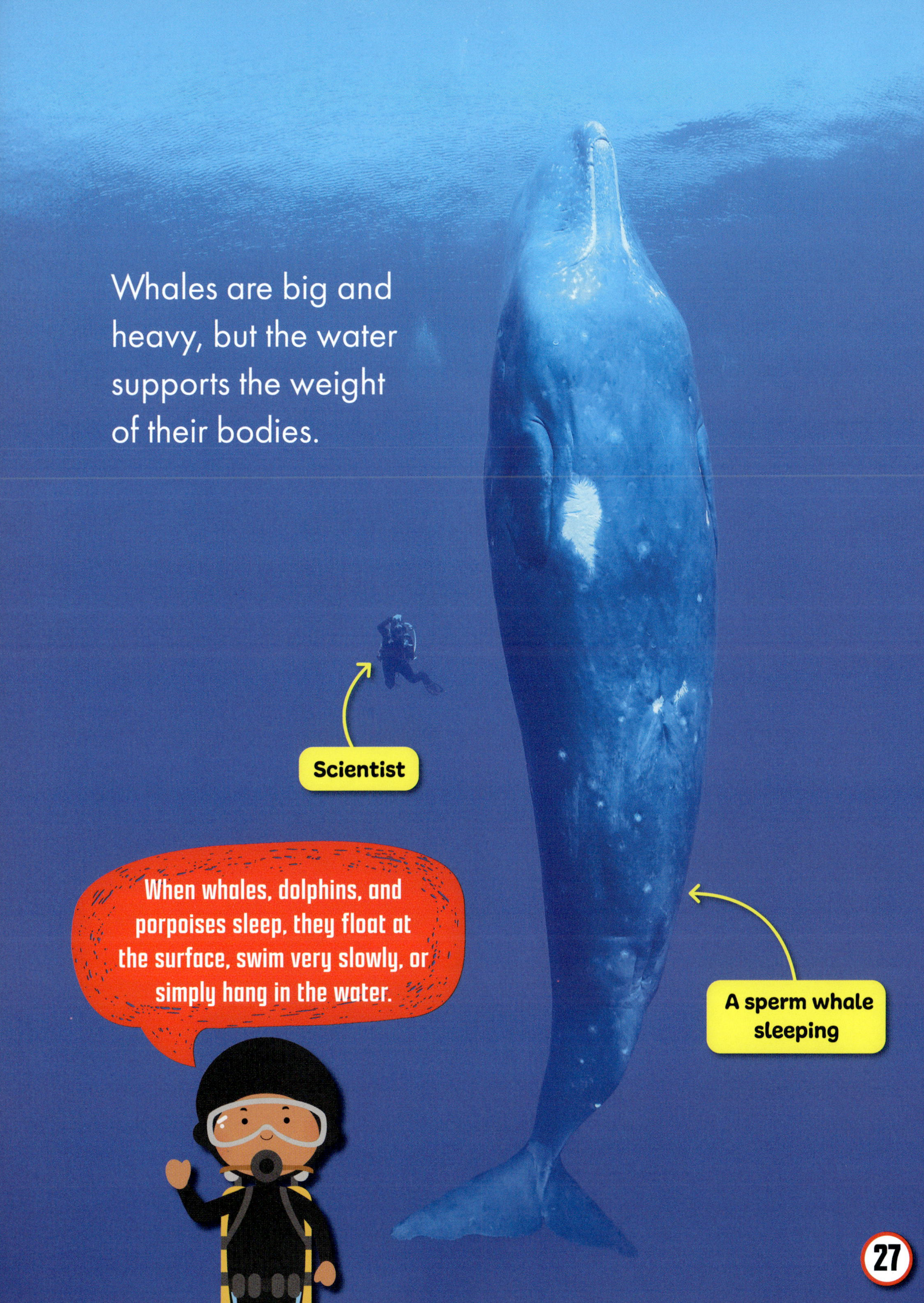
Whales are big and heavy, but the water supports the weight of their bodies.
Scientist
When whales, dolphins, and porpoises sleep, they float at the surface, swim very slowly, or simply hang in the water.
A sperm whale sleeping

Who Is the Fastest Swimmer?

Dolphins and porpoises are the speediest swimmers.

A dall's porpoise makes a big splash as it speeds along at 34 miles per hour (55 kilometers per hour).

Dall's porpoise

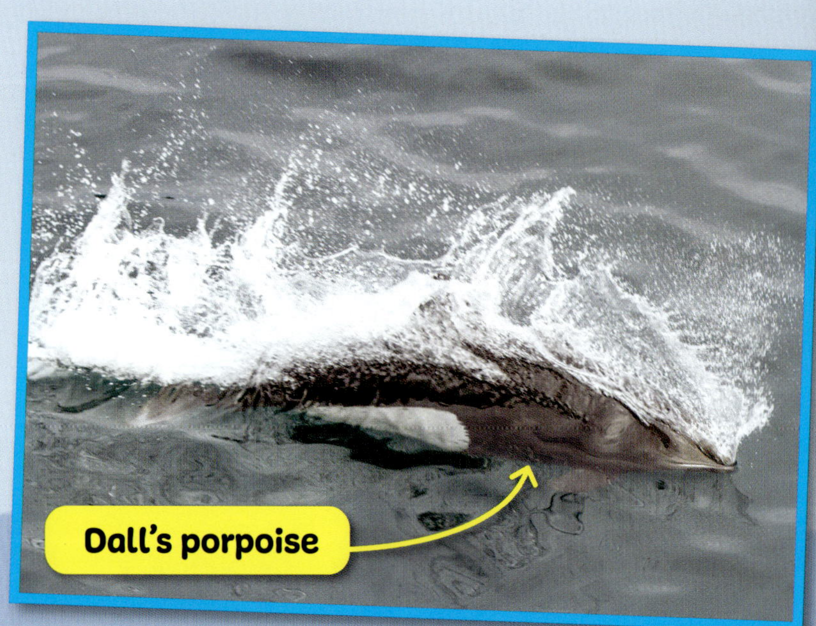

Orcas swim at 35 mph (56 km/h).

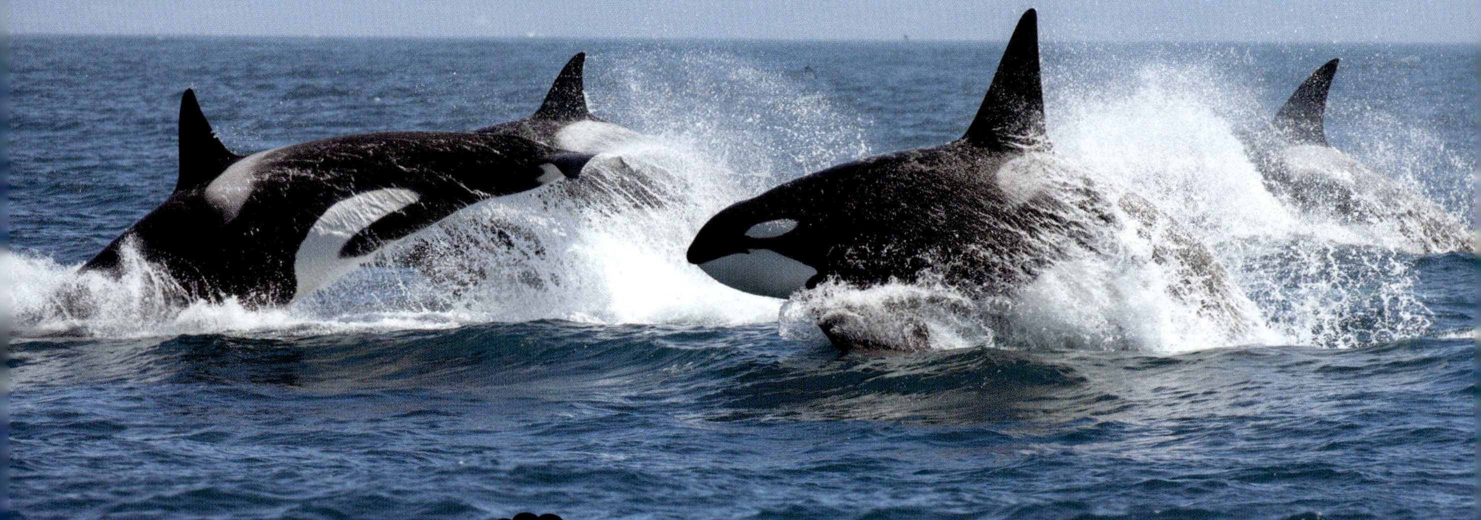

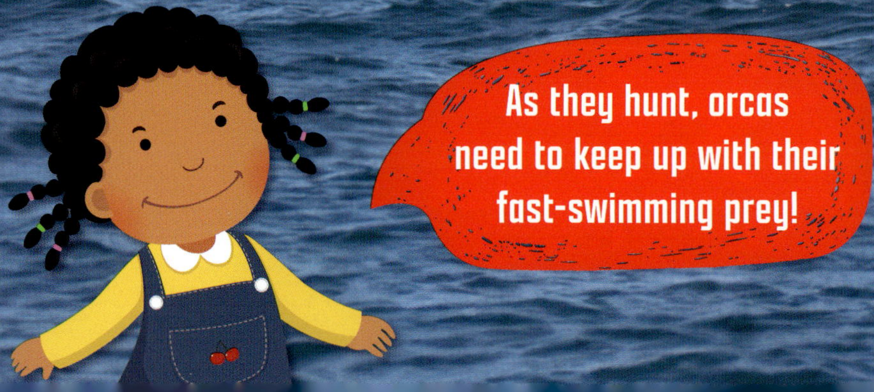
As they hunt, orcas need to keep up with their fast-swimming prey!

A sei whale can swim at more than 30 mph (48 km/h).

A right whale only swims at about 6 mph (10 km/h).

Right whale

But it can stay underwater for 40 minutes.

Who Has the Biggest Tail, Fin, and Flippers?

The humpback whale holds the record for the biggest tail.

The tail, or fluke, is made up of two parts called lobes.

A humpback whale's tail can be 18 feet (5.5 m) wide.

The dorsal fin on the backs of whales and dolphins helps balance them in the water.

Orcas have the tallest dorsal fin of any whale or dolphin.

The humpback whale also has the longest flippers.

The lumps on the flippers are called tubercles.

They help the whale make twists and turns in the water.

The flipper can be up to 15 feet (5 m) long!

How Does the Whale Family Breathe?

Like all mammals, whales, dolphins, and porpoises breathe the air.

They swim up to the water's surface and breathe through the blowholes on their heads.

Dolphin

Closed blowhole

Blowholes do the same job as your nostrils.

When they are underwater, they close their blowholes to keep water from getting in.

All the members of this animal group can go without breathing for a long time.
This helps them hunt for food.
15 MINUTES
Orca
Bottlenose dolphin
10 MINUTES
How Long Can They Hold Their Breath?
Humpback whale
Blue whale
20 MINUTES
20 MINUTES
A record-breaking Cuvier's beaked whale once held its breath for an incredible 3 hours and 42 minutes!
Cuvier's beaked whale
45 MINUTES
Sperm whale
60 MINUTES

Why Do Whales, Dolphins, and Porpoises Spout?

Before they breathe in, whales, dolphins, and porpoises breathe out the old air inside their bodies.

This is called spouting or blowing.

Different whales have differently shaped spouts.

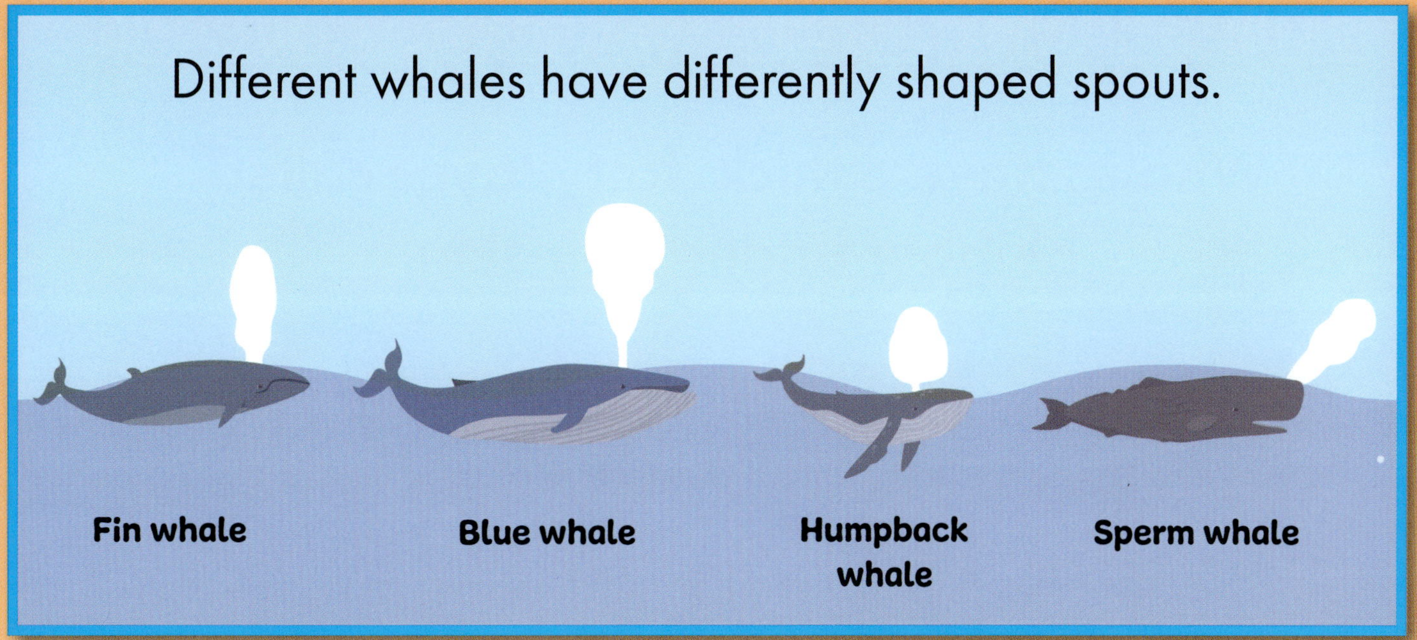

The biggest spout belongs to the blue whale.

Blue whale's spout

A blue whale's spout can reach 30 feet (9 m) into the air!

How Do Whales Keep Warm?

Whales have a thick, fatty layer called blubber under their skin.

This helps keep their body heat from escaping into the cold water.

Whales that live in icy water have the thickest blubber.

Dolphins and porpoises also have blubber.

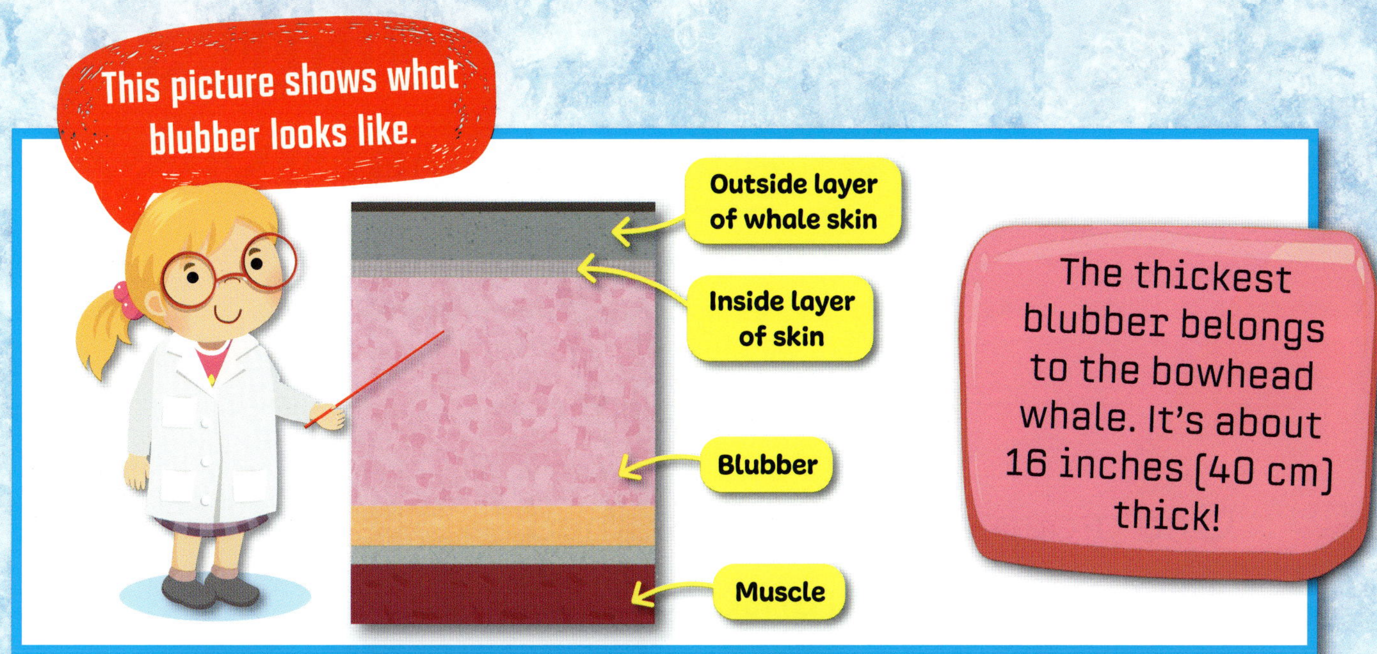

Blubber also helps a whale float.

This makes swimming less work for big animals.

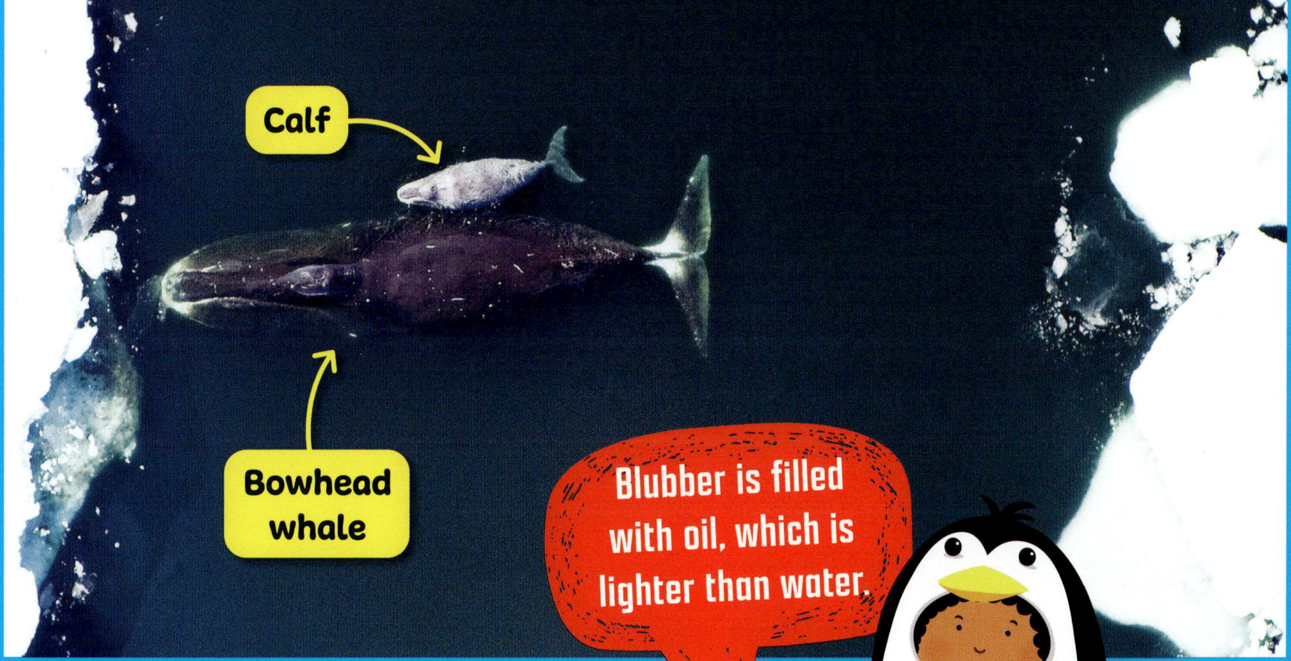

Calf

Bowhead whale

Blubber is filled with oil, which is lighter than water.

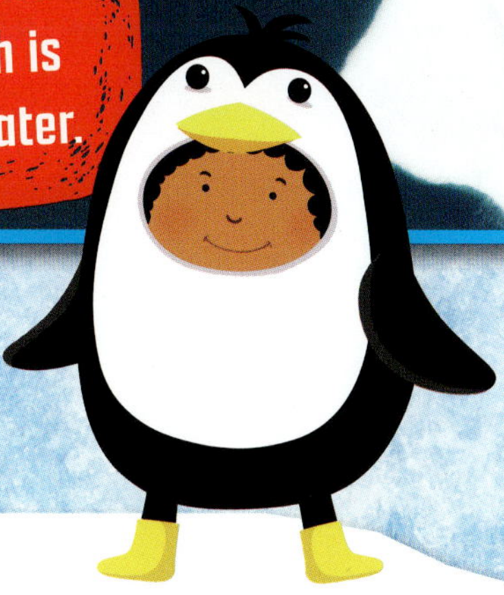

How Smart Are Whales, Dolphins, and Porpoises?

They are super-smart!

One group of orcas has learned a clever way to surprise seals.

The orcas hide in the waves close to shore.

Then they let the waves wash them onto the beach so they can grab seals.

Scientists have seen some dolphins with sea sponges on their snouts.

They use them to get to fish that hide in holes on the seabed.

Sea sponge

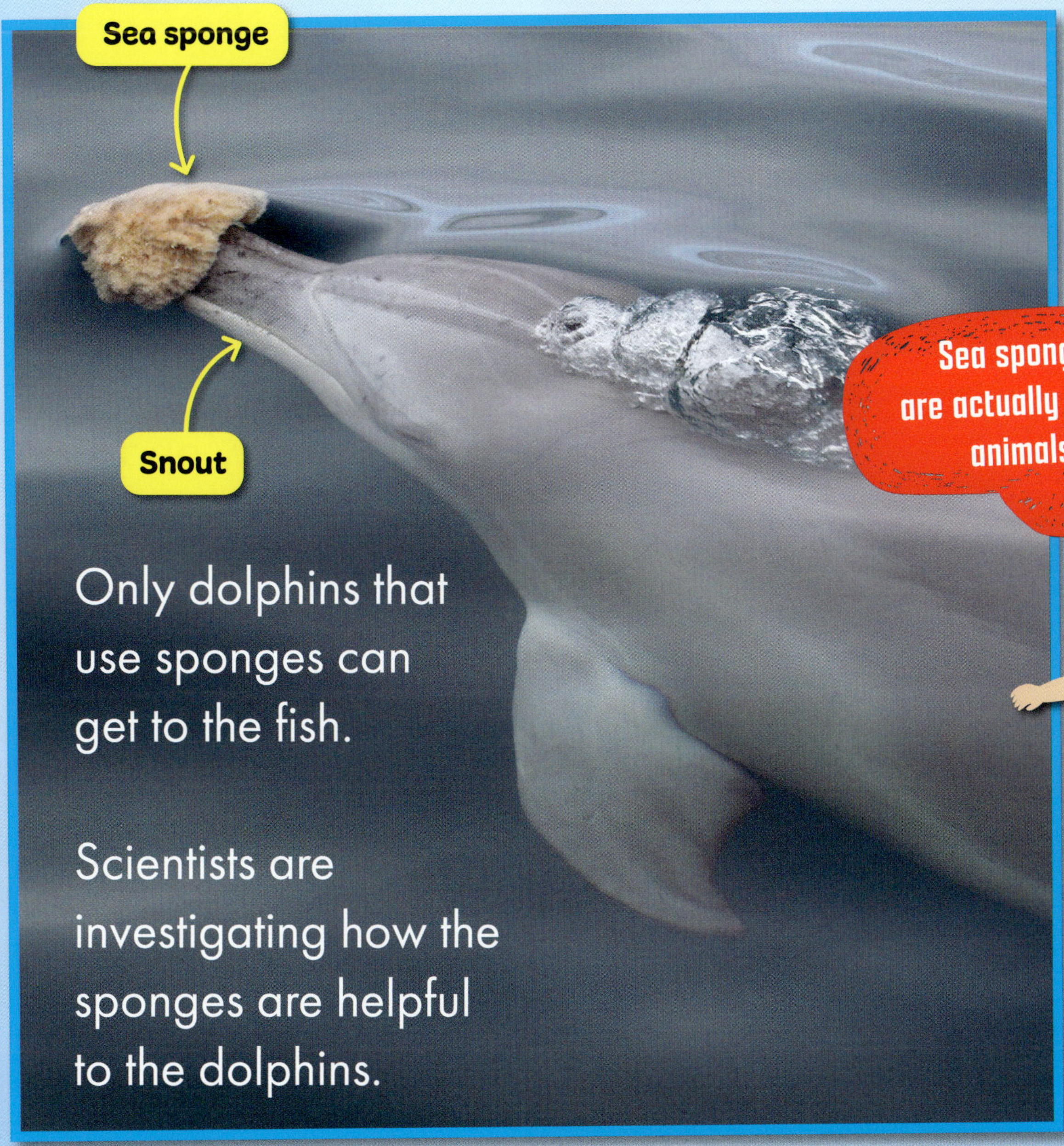

Snout

Only dolphins that use sponges can get to the fish.

Scientists are investigating how the sponges are helpful to the dolphins.

Sea sponges are actually ocean animals!

Who Grabs Food with Their Teeth?

Toothed whales do!

Dolphins, orcas, and sperm whales use their teeth to grab slippery prey such as fish and squid.

Dolphins grab fish and swallow them whole.

Orcas use their teeth to rip big prey apart, so they can swallow it in chunks.

An orca has about 50 teeth.

They swallow small fish and penguins in one gulp!

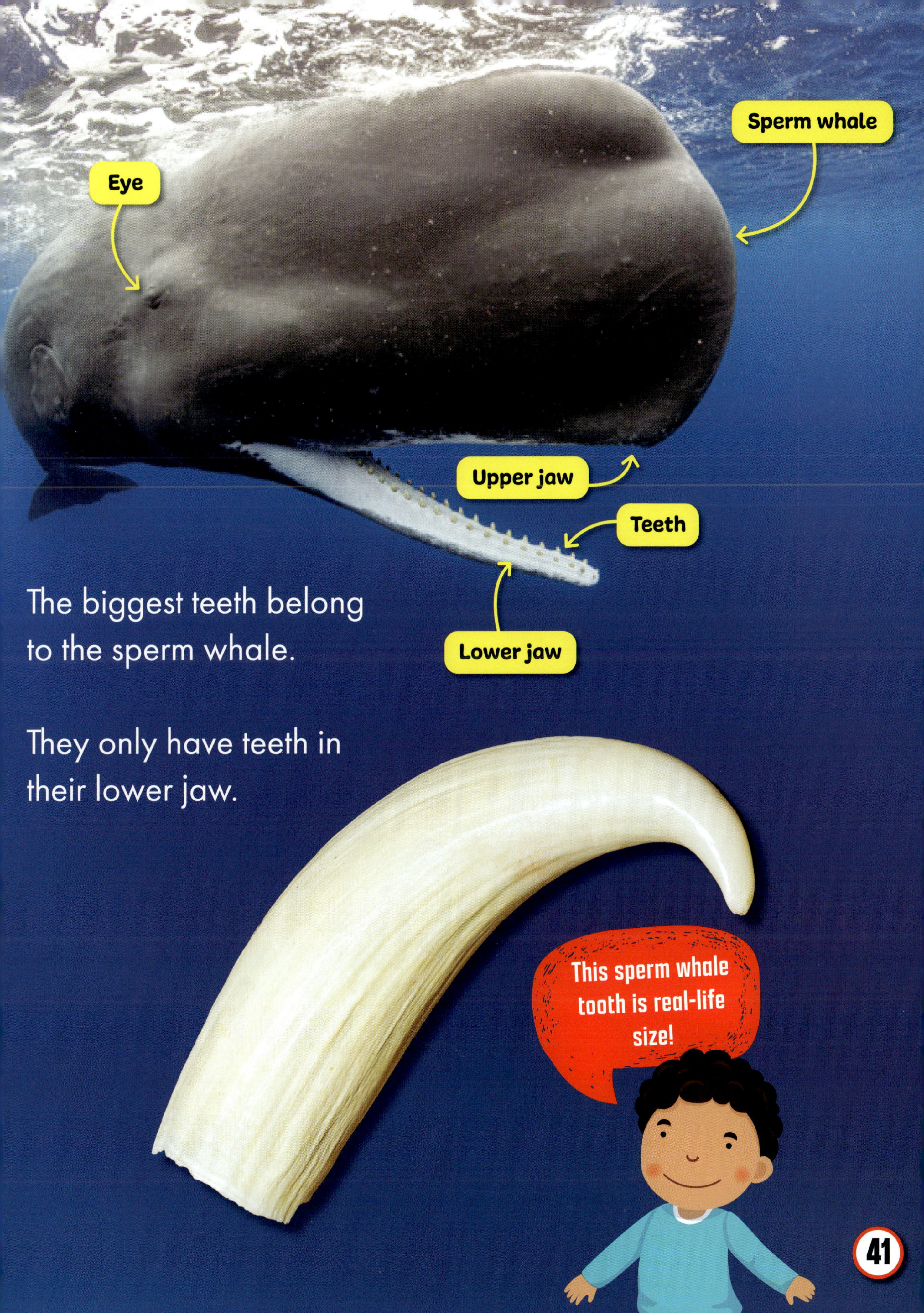

The biggest teeth belong to the sperm whale.

They only have teeth in their lower jaw.

Who Finds Food with Echoes?

Toothed whales, such as dolphins, have a clever way of locating, or finding, prey. It's called echolocation.

Long-beaked common dolphin

It's not possible to see in dark, murky water.

Toothed whales have a fatty area in their heads called the melon. They use it for echolocation.

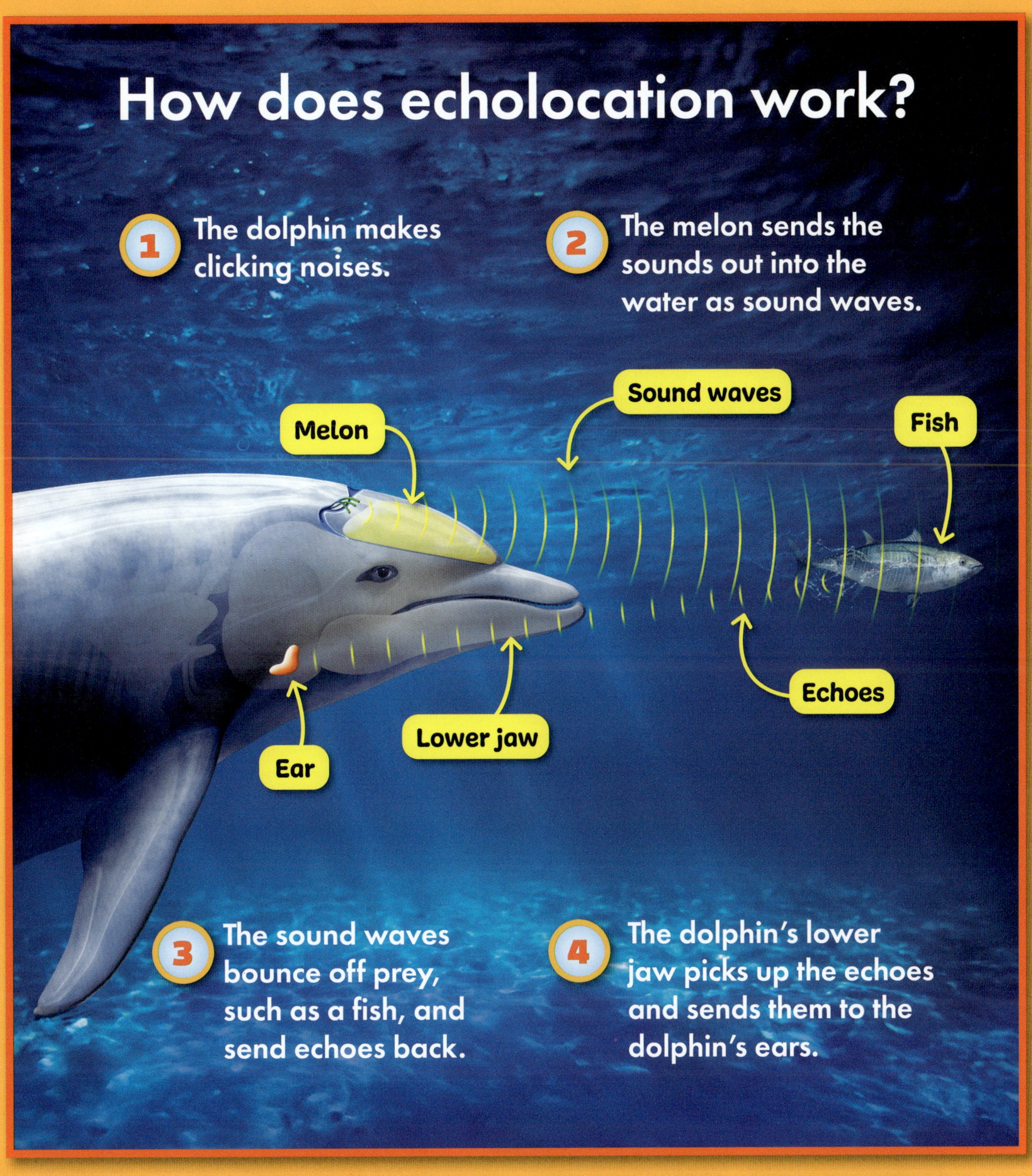

The echoes tell the dolphin where the fish is, how big it is, and even what speed it's moving at!

Who Hunts Giant Squid for Dinner?

The giant squid has eight arms, two long tentacles, and a sharp, beaky mouth.

This deep-sea creature is the favorite food of the sperm whale.

A sperm whale eating a giant squid

Tentacle

Sperm whales dive almost 2 miles (3.2 km) under the ocean to hunt giant squid.

Colossal squid beak

Sperm whales also eat the colossal squid.

Its hard beak has been found in the stomachs of dead sperm whales.

How Does a Sperm Whale Dive So Deep?

The sperm whale is a champion diver.

Sperm whale spouting

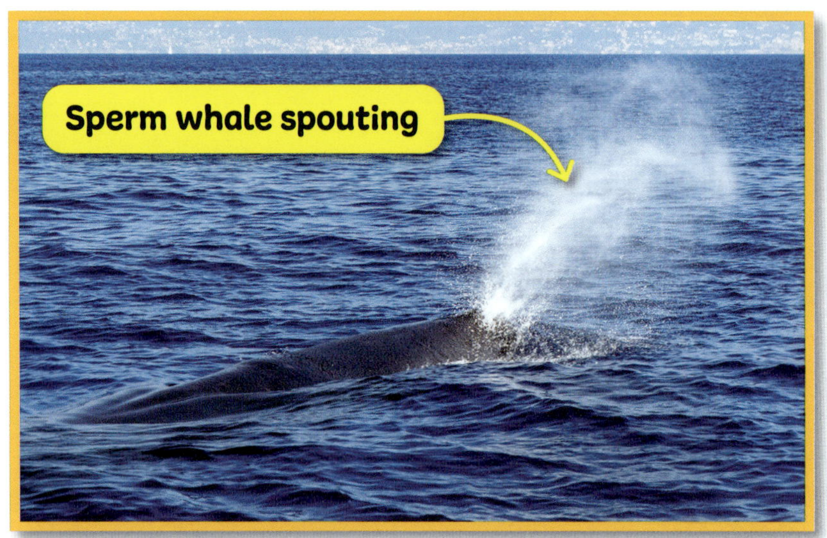

It takes a big breath of air with its blowhole before a dive.

Deep under the ocean, the weight of all the water presses down on the sperm whale.

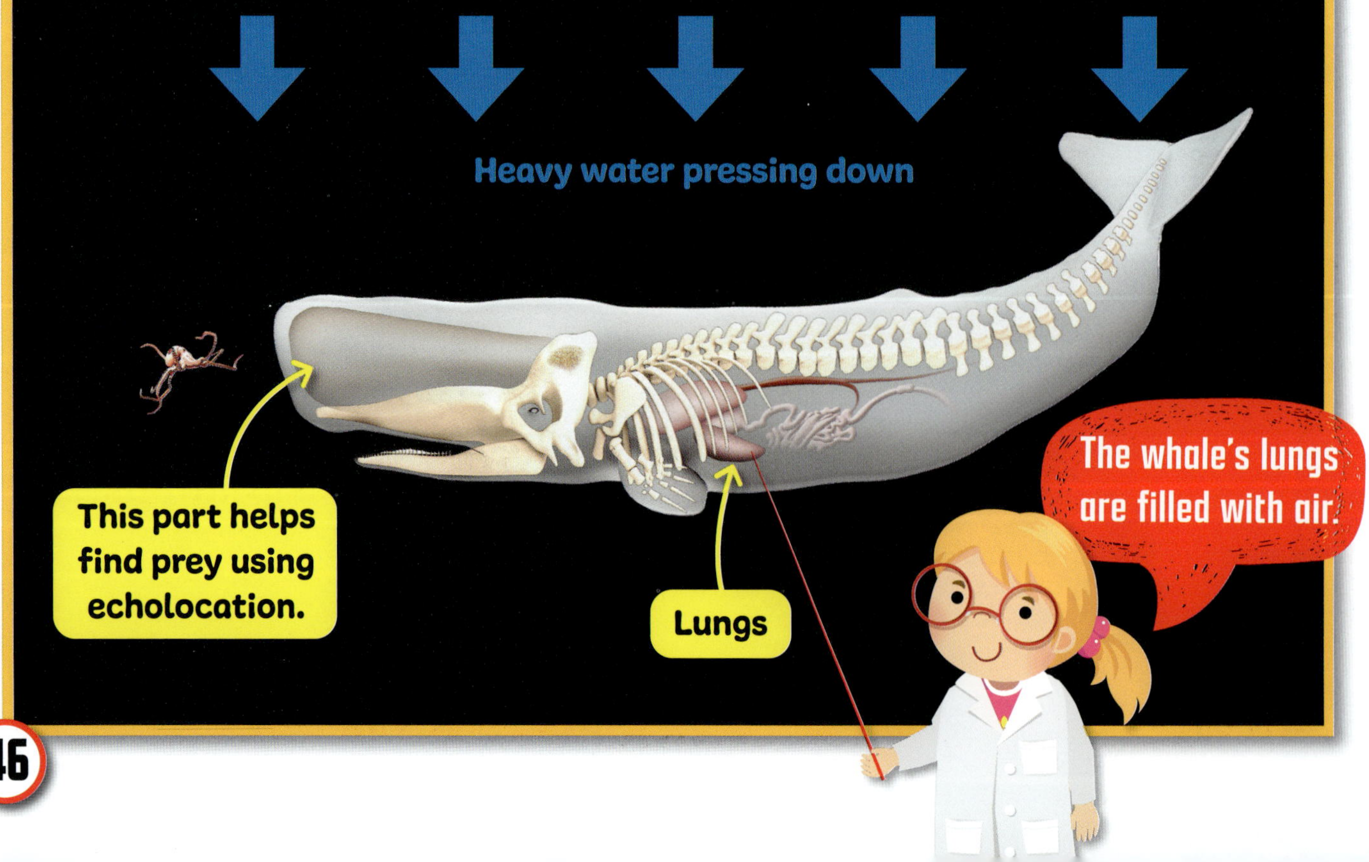
Heavy water pressing down
This part helps find prey using echolocation.
Lungs
The whale's lungs are filled with air.

The heavy water pressing down on the whale could pop its air-filled lungs—like squeezing a balloon.

To protect its lungs, the whale collapses, or squishes, them down.

It still needs oxygen from the air to keep its body working.

So the oxygen is stored in the whale's blood and muscles.

Who Are the Wolves of the Ocean?

Orcas are nicknamed "wolves of the ocean."

They live in family groups and hunt together, just like a pack of wolves on land.

An orca family

Orcas come to the surface to spyhop.

They look for other orcas, boats, and prey.

Orcas have a clever way to catch seals.

They swim together to make a big wave.

Orcas hunt seals, sealions, fish, and other whales. Some even attack great white sharks.

The wave washes a seal off the ice, so the orcas can catch it!

Why Are Orcas Black and White?

The patterns on orcas help them hide from prey.

Their black body blends in with dark water.

Look at this picture. The orcas' white markings make it hard for prey animals to see their shapes.

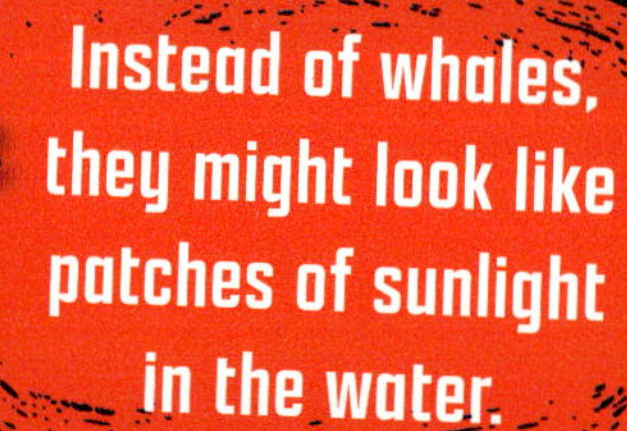

Hiding with colors or patterns is called **camouflage**.

All orcas have the same pattern.

But each orca's white markings are just a tiny bit different.

This may help family members recognize each other.

How Do Beluga Whales Stay Safe?

To keep safe from predators, beluga whales use camouflage.

Mother belugas give birth to their babies in places where rivers meet the ocean.

The water here can be dark, muddy, and cloudy.

So baby belugas are born gray.

Adult belugas live in icy, frozen water.

They must come to holes in the ice to breathe.

But hungry polar bears could be waiting to attack!

So belugas turn white as they grow up to blend in with their icy home.

Who Is the Unicorn of the Ocean?

It's the narwhal. This whale has a long, spiral tusk—like a unicorn's horn!

An illustration of a narwhal

A narwhal has just two teeth. As one tooth grows, it breaks through the narwhal's lip.

It becomes a tusk that measures 10 feet (3 m) long.

Scientists don't know for sure why narwhals have tusks.

These males are rubbing their tusks together.

They could be figuring out who's the biggest and strongest.

How Do Baleen Plates Work?

When it feeds, a baleen whale takes in a huge mouthful of water.

Then it pushes the water back out through its baleen plates with its tongue.

The baleen plates trap millions of tiny animals that are in the water.

Then the animals are swallowed!

The tiny animals that baleen whales eat are called **zooplankton**.

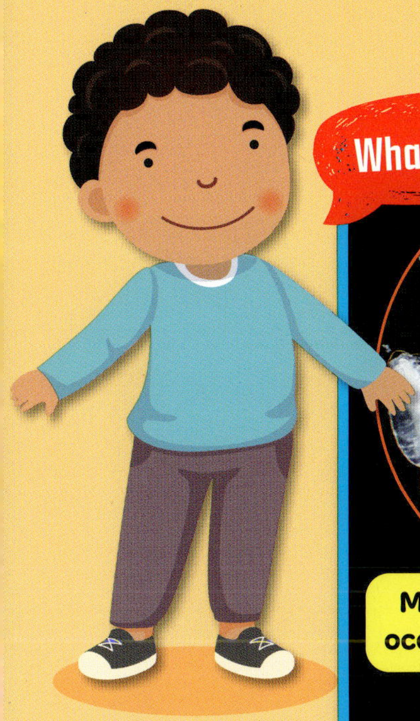

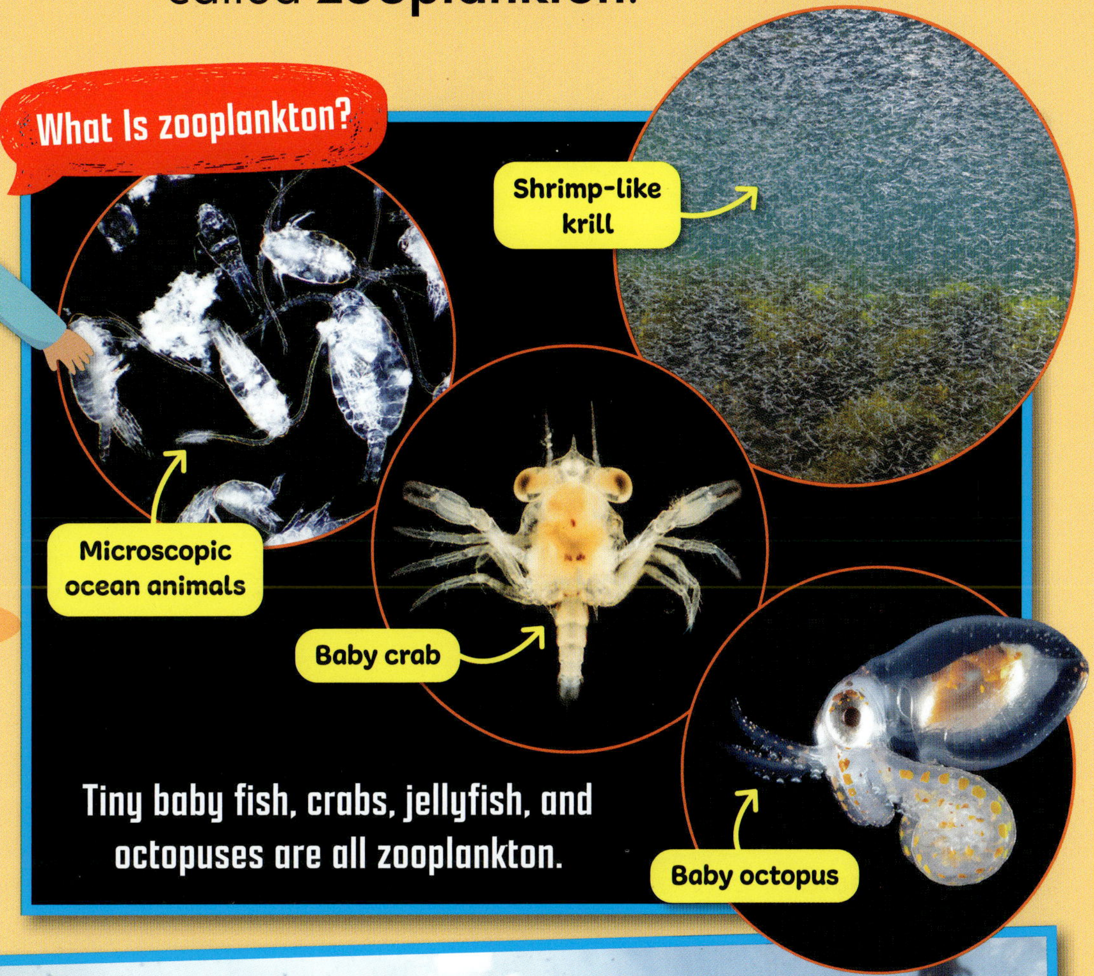
What Is zooplankton?
Shrimp-like krill
Microscopic ocean animals
Baby crab
Baby octopus

Tiny baby fish, crabs, jellyfish, and octopuses are all zooplankton.

Blue whale poop

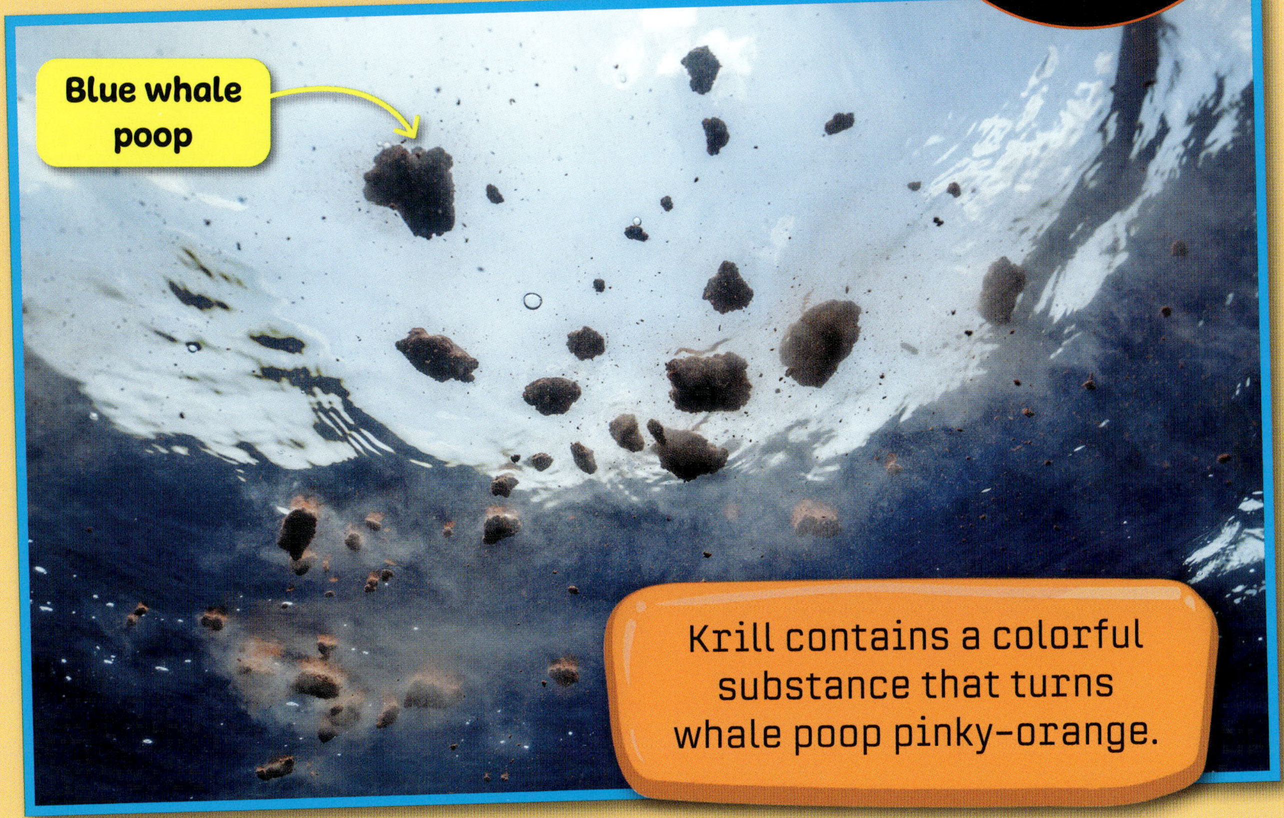

Krill contains a colorful substance that turns whale poop pinky-orange.

Who Has the Biggest Mouth?

The biggest mouth belongs to the bowhead whale.

Bowhead whales swim under ice in freezing water.

They use their giant heads to smash holes in the ice so they can breathe.

Bowhead whales have the longest baleen.

The baleen grows up to 13 feet (4 m) long.

Bowheads live longer than any other whale—up to 200 years!

Who Catches Food with Bubbles?

Humpback whales do! This is called bubble-netting.

A humpback releases air into the water from its blowhole.

It swims in a circle, making a net of bubbles.

The whale swirls the bubbles with its flippers.

Fish get trapped in the bubble net. Then the whale gulps them down!

In Alaska, humpback whales work as a team.

Some team members circle the fish to keep them from escaping.

Gulping down fish

Another team member blows a bubble net to trap the fish.

The whole team shares the feast!

Bubbles

Do Whales and Dolphins Stick Together?

Yes! Many types of whales and dolphins live in groups.

Dolphins form the biggest groups and have strong **bonds**.

They help each other find food, keep safe from predators, and raise their young.

Female sperm whales form family groups with their calves.
A group might include mothers, daughters, and aunts.
The females take turns babysitting, so the others can go hunting.
Female sperm whale babysitter
Calf
Sperm whale calves need protection from orcas and sharks.
Male sperm whales live alone or in male groups.

Why Do Whales Sing?

Baleen whales, such as blue whales, make humming, moaning sounds called whale song.

Their songs travel for hundreds of miles.

Whales sing to find mates and to communicate with other whales.

Male humpback whales can sing for hours!

Scientists have discovered that they copy each other's songs.

Which Whale Is a Long-Distance Traveler?

Some whales, dolphins, and porpoises swim long distances to find food and mates, and to give birth. This is called migration.

Gray whales migrate the farthest.

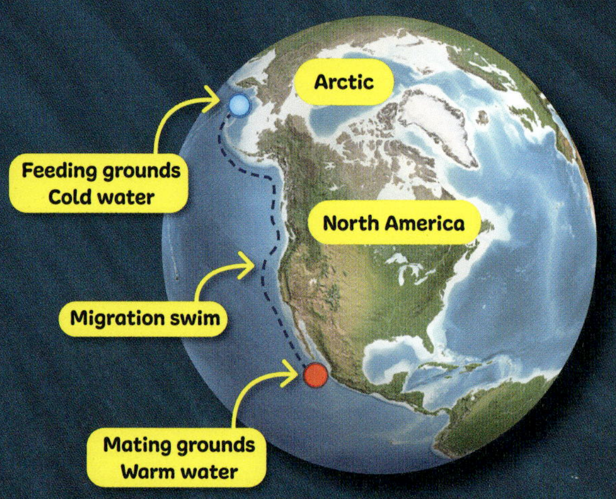

Each September, gray whales swim from the cold Arctic waters where they feed.

They head south to warmer waters to mate.

Then the whales swim back to the north.

A gray whale travels around 12,000 miles (19,000 km) every year!

Pregnant females, who mated last year, migrate south to give birth to their calves.

Mother whales wait in the warm water for their calves to get fat and strong.

Then the babies can make the long swim back to the north.

This tired calf is having a rest on its mom!

When it's summer in Antarctica, many whales migrate there to feast.

The icy waters are packed with whale food.

The ocean around Antarctica is clean and cold. It's the perfect place for lots of krill, fish, and squid to live.

Antarctica

Icy ocean

Antarctica

Humpback whale

Antarctic krill

Blue whales, humpback whales, fin whales, and minke whales migrate to feed on krill.

In summer, it's always daytime in Antarctica because the Sun never sets.

Minke whale

Orcas live around Antarctica all year.

They hunt seals, penguins, and the other whales that live there.

Are These Ocean Mammals Good Moms?

Yes! Whales, dolphins, and porpoises are great moms.

Calf

Southern right whale

After giving birth, they take care of their calves for many months. Sometimes even years!

A southern right whale is pregnant for 12 months.

An orca is pregnant for up to 18 months!

As soon as a calf is born, mom guides it up to the water's surface.

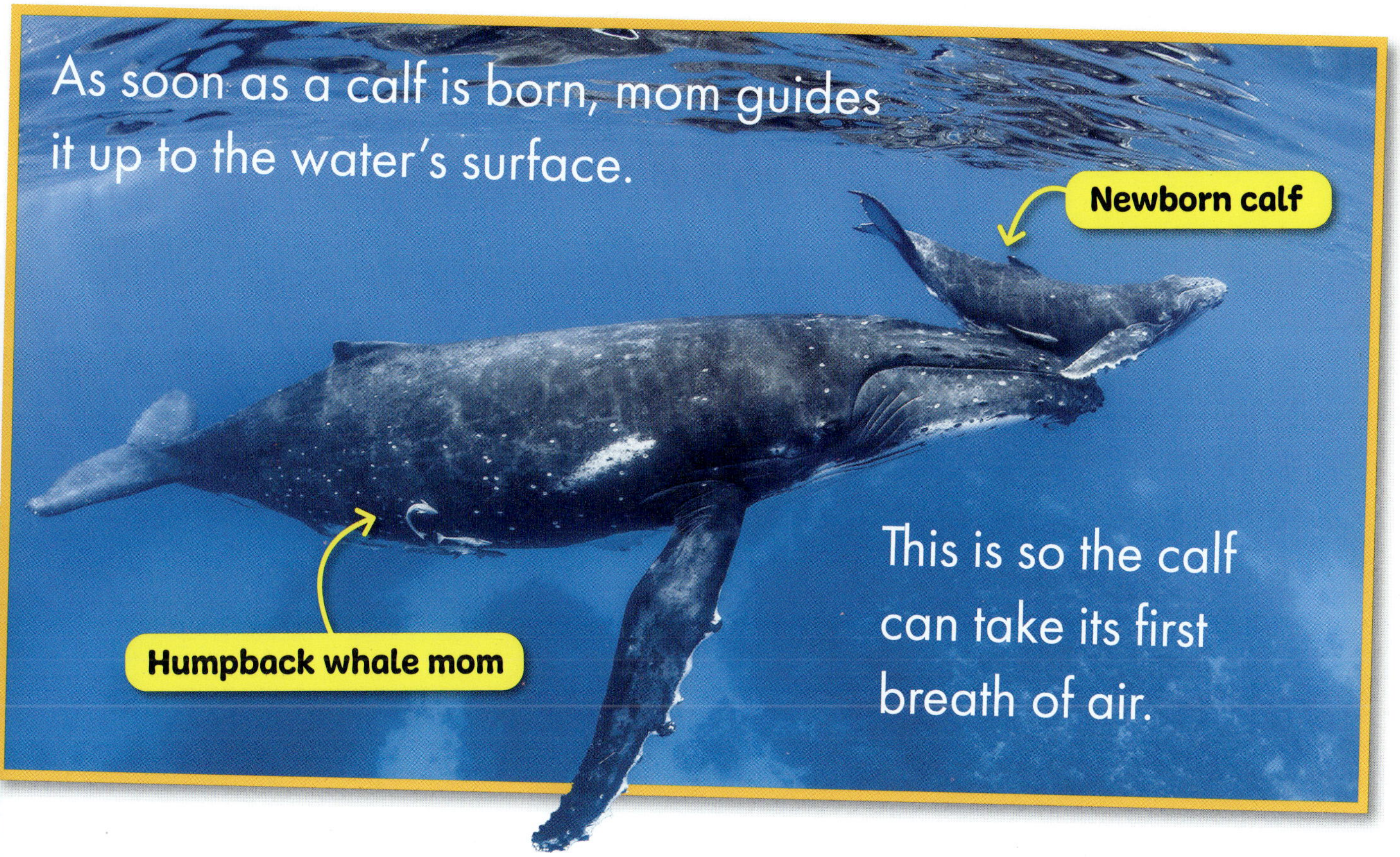

Newborn calf

Humpback whale mom

This is so the calf can take its first breath of air.

Living in a group helps protect dolphin calves from predators such as orcas and sharks.

Can you spot the dolphin calf?

Spinner dolphins

How Fast Does a Calf Grow?

Newborn whales and dolphins grow very fast.

They feed on their mother's milk, which is rich and fatty.

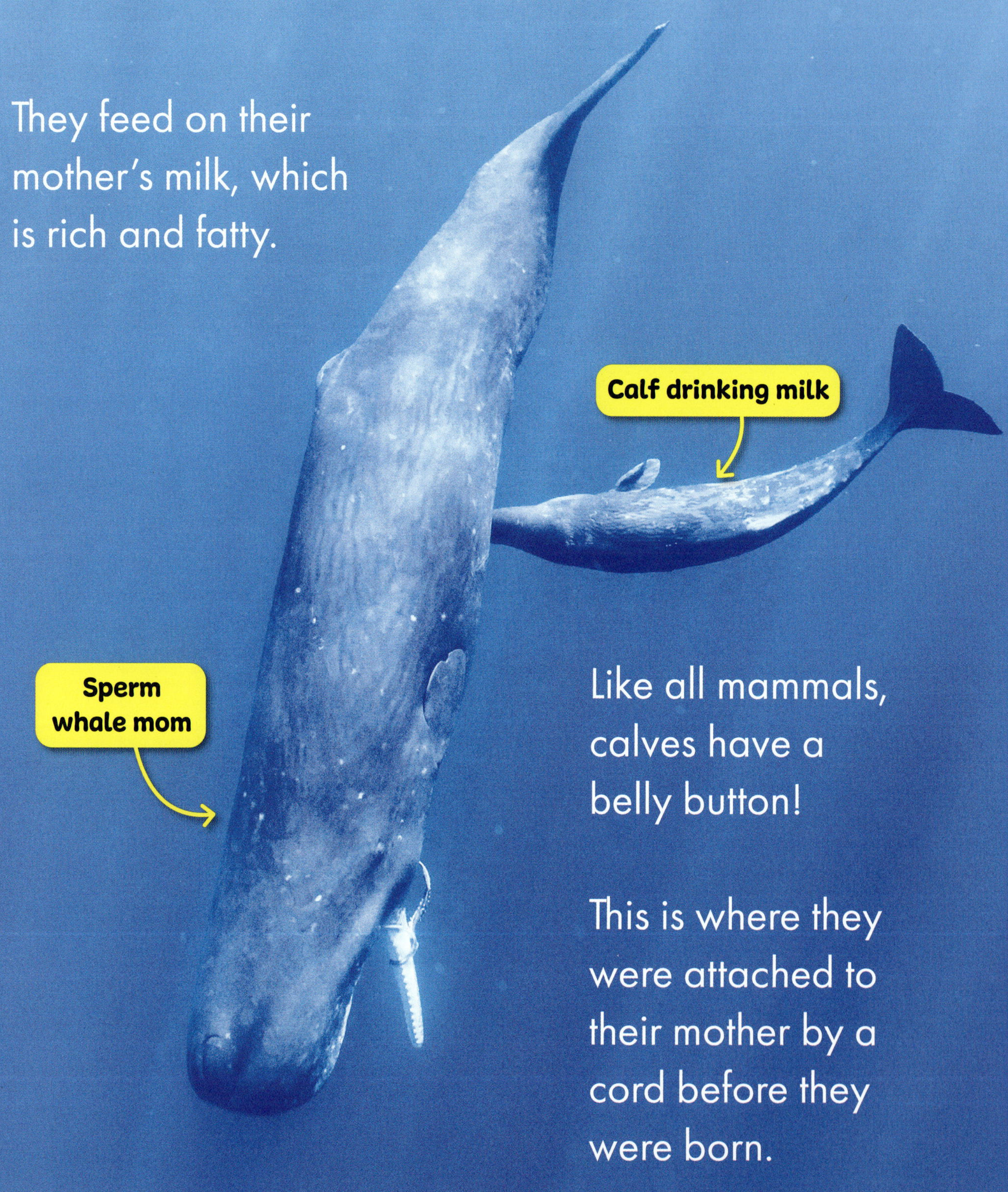

Like all mammals, calves have a belly button!

This is where they were attached to their mother by a cord before they were born.

A calf quickly gains weight and forms blubber to keep it warm.

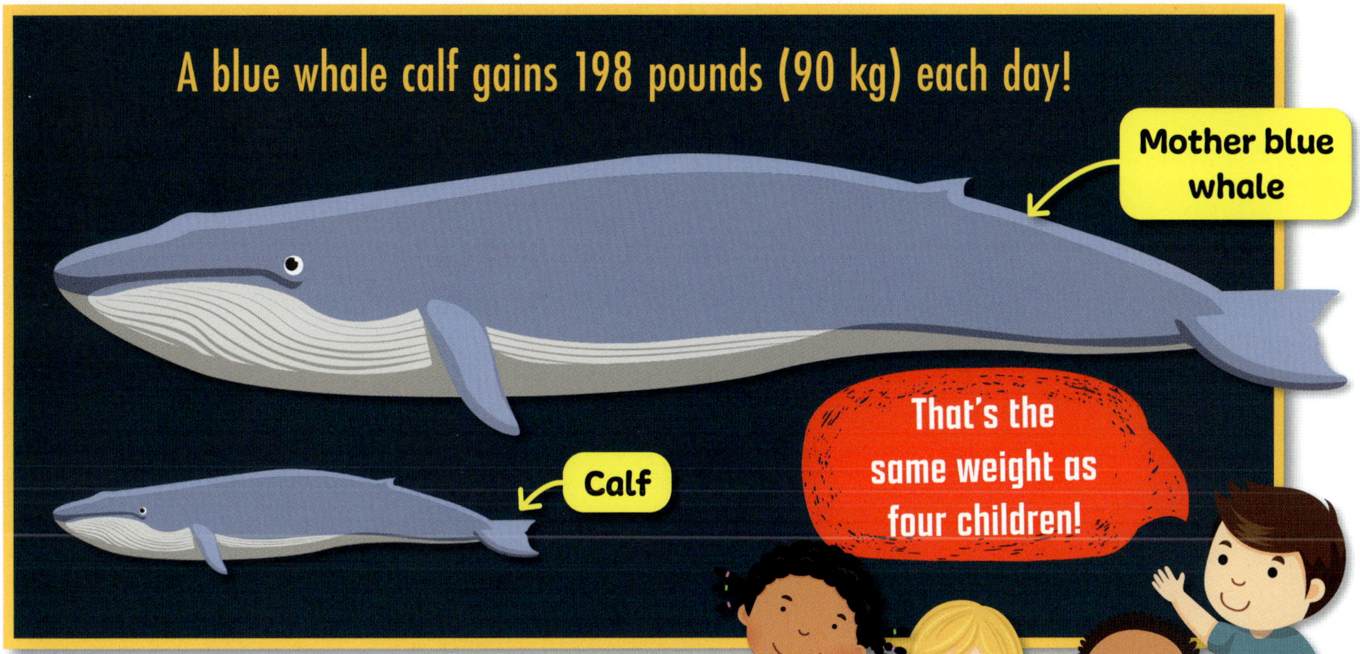
A blue whale calf gains 198 pounds (90 kg) each day!
Mother blue whale
Calf

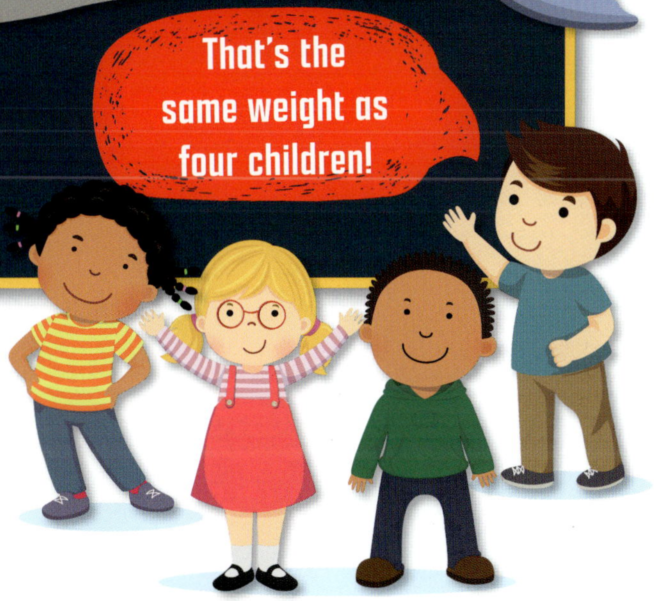
That's the same weight as four children!

Whales, dolphins, and porpoises are born with bristly whiskers.

One-day-old calf

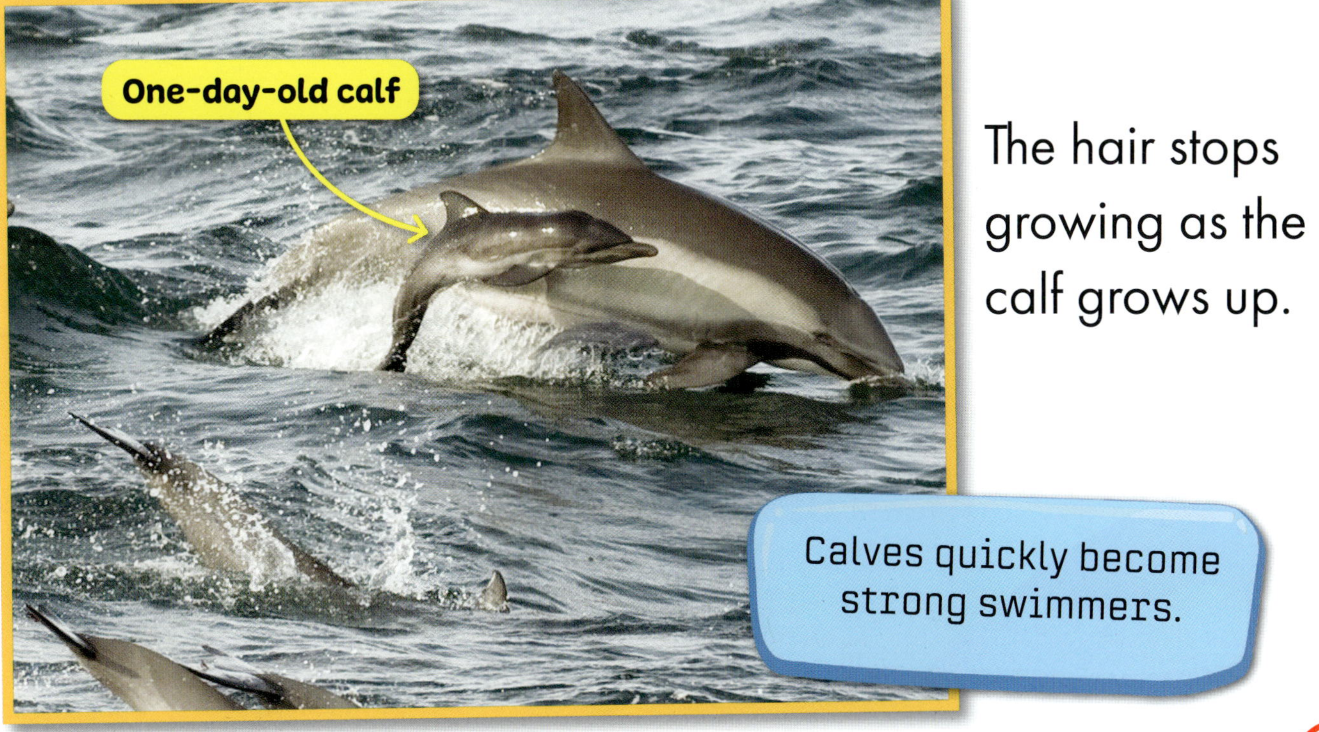

The hair stops growing as the calf grows up.

Calves quickly become strong swimmers.

Do Dolphins Live in Rivers?

Yes! Some dolphins do live in freshwater rivers.

River dolphins have large, rounded heads and long, beaky snouts.

The Ganges River dolphin is nearly blind.

However, the Ganges River is so muddy, the dolphin doesn't need to see.

It uses echolocation to find fish to eat.

The Ganges River dolphin is very rare. There may only be about 5,000 left!

There were once five different types of river dolphins.

But the Yangtze River dolphin became **extinct** in 2007.

Which River Dolphin Turns Pink?

It's the Amazon River dolphin. These dolphins are born gray. But they slowly turn pink as they grow older.

Amazon River dolphin

Pink skin

Male Amazon River dolphins are pinker than females.

North America

The Amazon River dolphin lives here.

Amazon Rain Forest

South America

They hunt for fish, crabs, and turtles in the Amazon River.

The river flows through the Amazon Rain Forest.

Trees growing
in floodwater

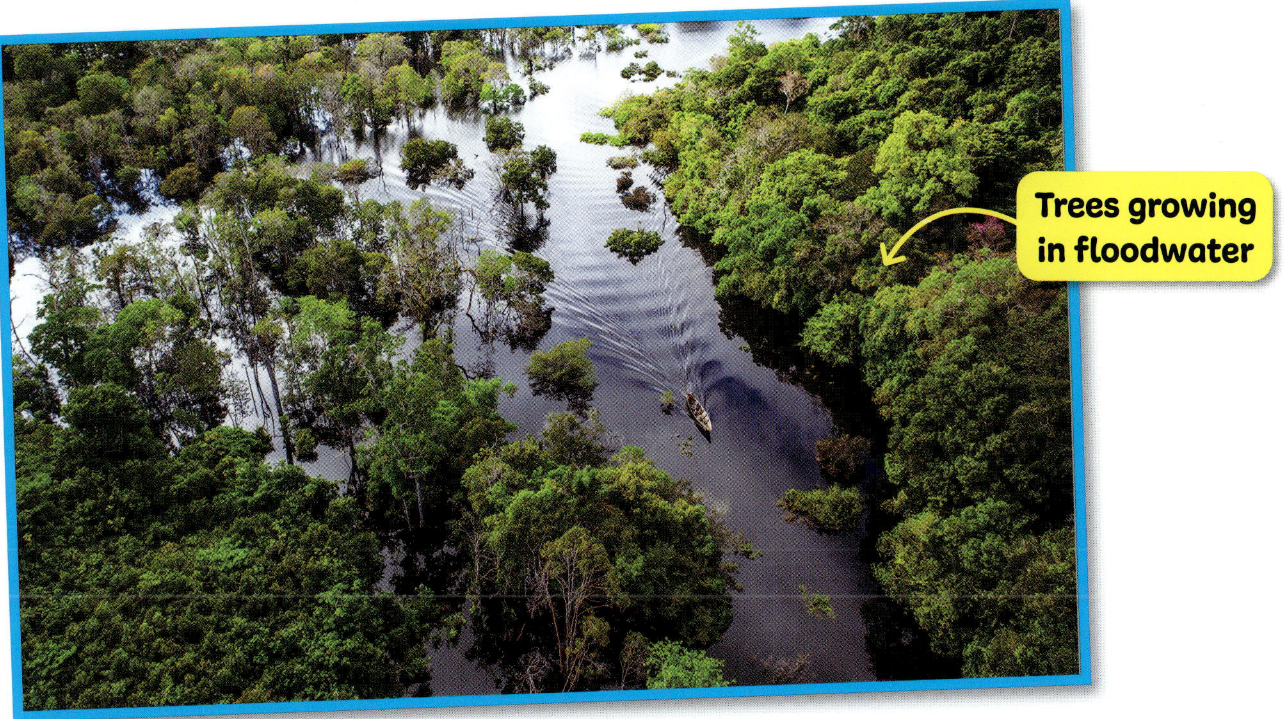

Sometimes there is so much rain, the river overflows and floods the forest.

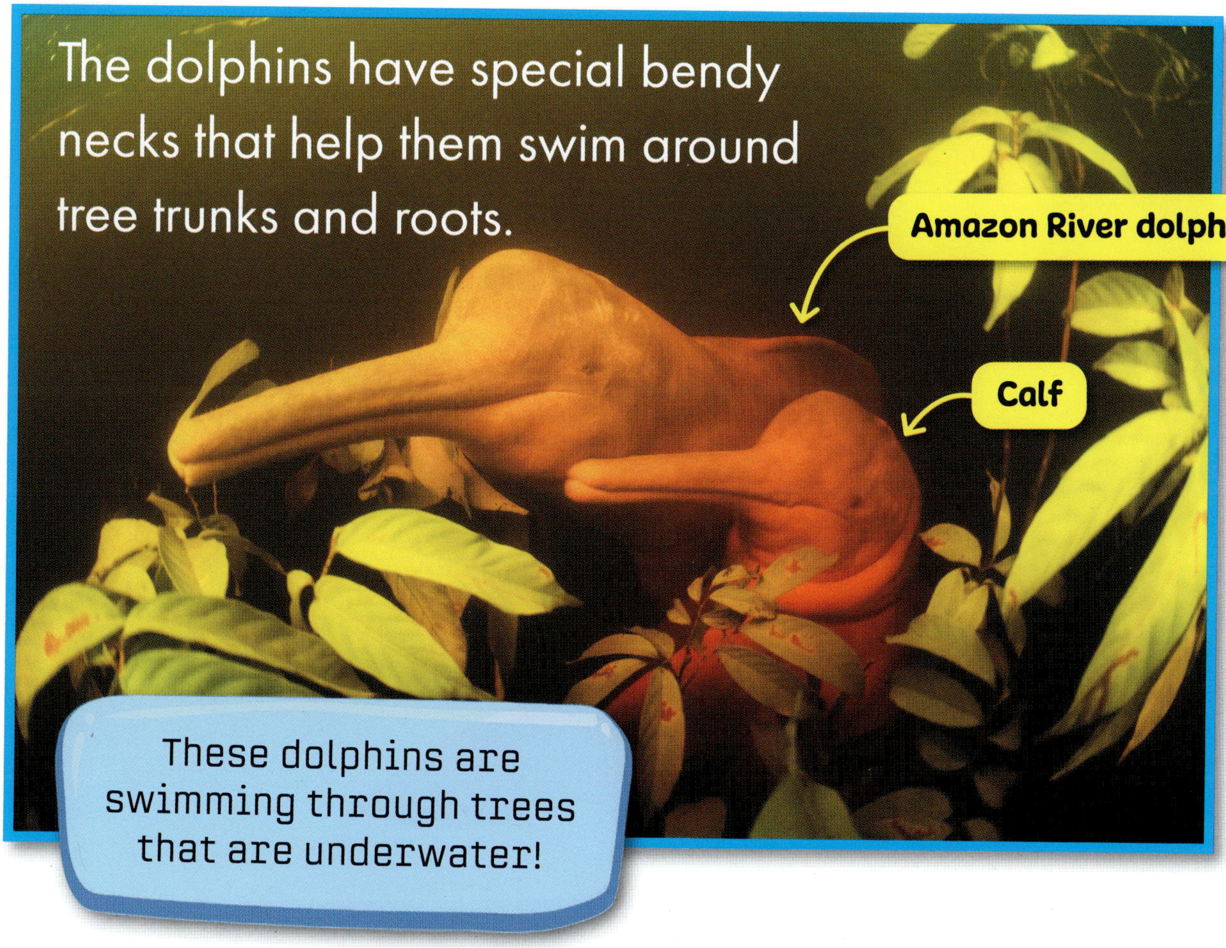
The dolphins have special bendy
necks that help them swim around
tree trunks and roots.
Amazon River dolphin
Calf
These dolphins are
swimming through trees
that are underwater!

What Do Whale Scientists Do?

They follow, watch, and carefully study whales, dolphins, and porpoises.

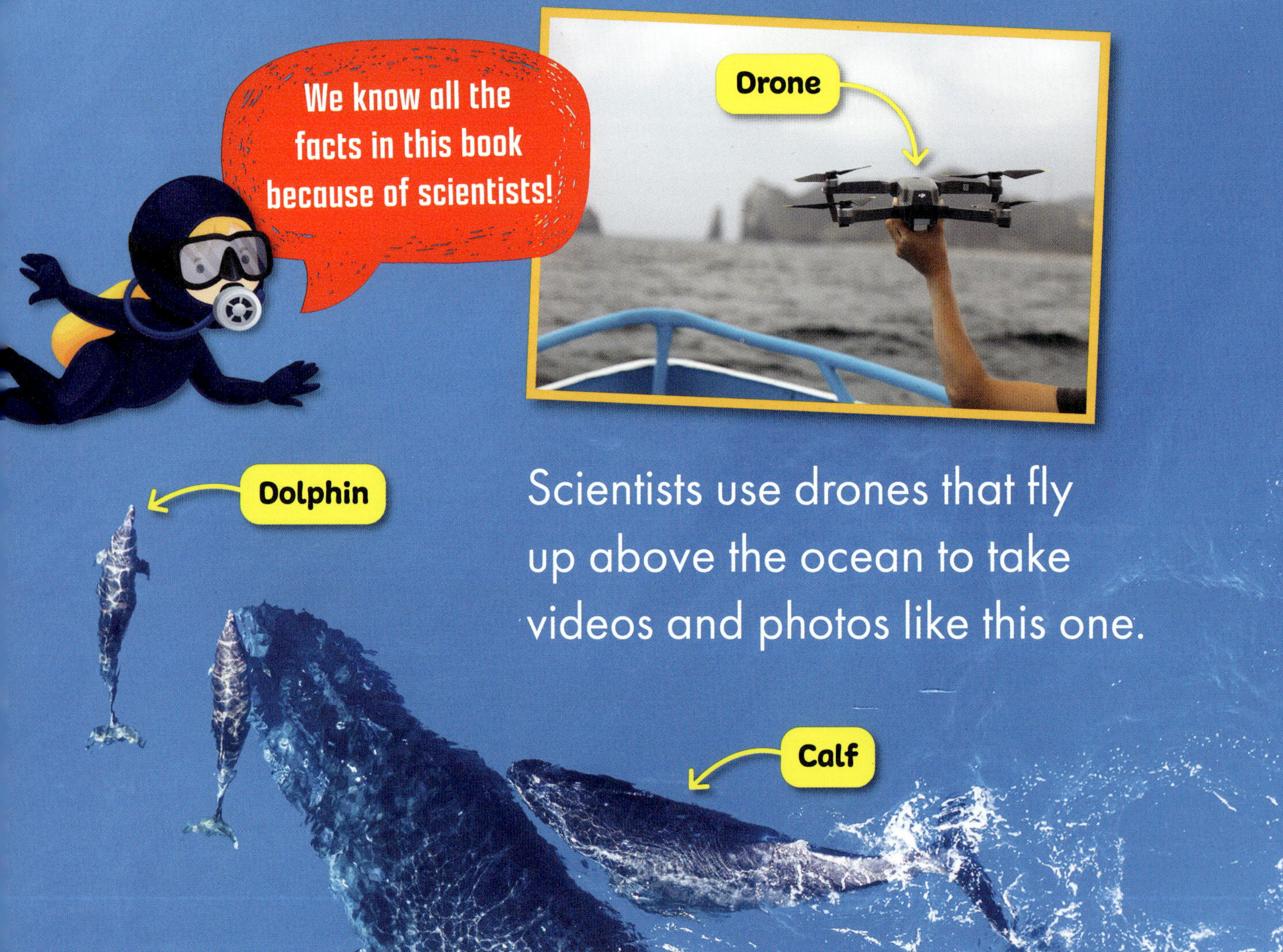

Scientists use drones that fly up above the ocean to take videos and photos like this one.

Mother humpback whale

Scientists attach tags, or **tracking devices**, to the animals' backs.

A tag sends information to scientists, such as where a whale travels.

Scientists call the members of this amazing animal family cetaceans.

A scientist who studies cetaceans is called a cetologist.

Let's say it!
"seh-tai-shuns"

Can I Spot a Whale or Dolphin?

If you're lucky, you might one day spot a whale!

There are companies that take people on whale and dolphin-spotting boat trips.

If you are on vacation or visiting the seashore, you might get the chance to take a trip.

It's also possible to spot whales and dolphins from land.

There are places on some coasts where they swim close to land.

Keep watch on the water. Look for a dark shape, a tail, or a flipper!

Are Whales and Dolphins Friendly?

Whales and dolphins are intelligent animals. They are also very curious. This makes them seem friendly to us.

However, they are still wild animals. We should not go up to them or touch them.

If you are lucky enough to see whales, dolphins, or porpoises, stay calm and quiet.

This gray whale has swum close to a boat. It is having a good look at these whale-watchers.

Dolphins enjoy riding the bow waves made by boats and ships.

Bow of ship

Long-beaked common dolphin

Bow wave

Scientists sometimes take photos and videos of whales and dolphins underwater.

Scientist

Southern right whale

Scientists are careful not to get too close.

How Does Whale Poop Help Our Planet?

Get ready for some BIG science!

Our lovely planet is getting too warm because of harmful gases in the air. One of these gases is called carbon dioxide.

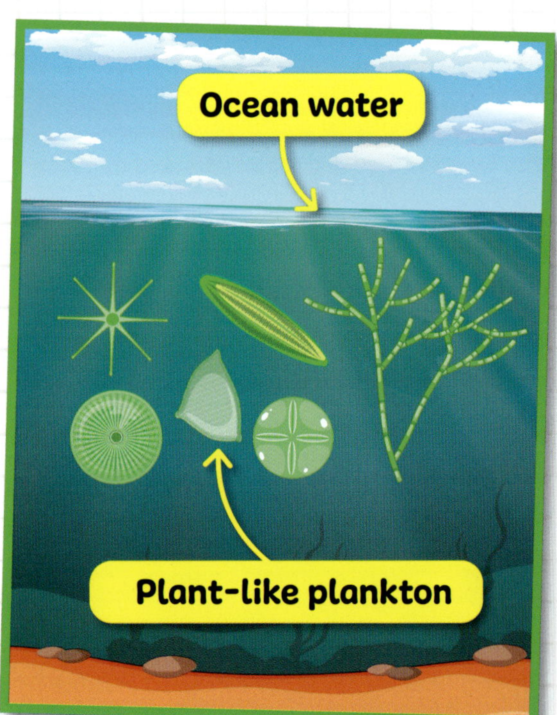

Tiny, green, plant-like **plankton** that live in the ocean can help.

They soak up carbon dioxide and take it out of the air!

Whale poop contains lots of nutrients, or goodness, that plankton need.

The tiny plankton soak up the nutrients from the water.

Whale poop

Sperm whales

Plant-like plankton

The nutrients keep the plankton healthy and help make more plankton.

How Do Whales Help Other Animals?

When a whale dies, its giant body falls to the seabed.

The body becomes a busy habitat called a "whale fall."

A tiger shark feeding

A hagfish

Sharks, hagfish, and other big animals tear the body apart to eat the meat.

Octopuses, eels, sea cucumbers, clams, and other animals also gather to feed.

Octopus

Eel

Sea cucumber

Clams

After about 10 years, all that's left are bones.

Then tiny bone-eating worms tunnel into the bones to feed.

Whale skeleton

Octopus

A whale's body can feed lots of animals for up to 50 years!

Why Are Whales, Dolphins, and Porpoises in Danger?

Like many ocean creatures, this animal family is in danger because of the actions of people.

Some people drop trash on beaches. Then it gets washed out to sea.

Ocean animals eat the harmful trash, thinking it is food.

Oil gets spilled from ships and poisons ocean water.

Dirty water is pumped into rivers and flows out to sea.

Whales, dolphins, and porpoises get caught up and hurt in fishing nets.

This fishing net might keep the whale from swimming to the surface to breathe.

Large, noisy ships travel in the places where whales migrate. This disturbs the whales and keeps them from swimming to the places where they feed and have their calves.

There may be fewer than 10 vaquita porpoises left in the ocean. That's because so many have died in fishing nets.

How Can I Help Whales, Dolphins, and Porpoises?

There are lots of ways!
Get your friends and family to join in, too.

Never drop trash. It could end up in a river or the ocean.

Adopt a whale, dolphin, or porpoise with a charity. The money you pay will help protect these animals.

Try to use less plastic. Recycle plastic trash when you can.

Never visit aquariums that keep whales or dolphins. They should be living free in the ocean!

Go on a beach clean-up with your family.

One day, you might get the chance to go whale-watching or dolphin-spotting.

Ask your grown-ups to choose a company that follows strict rules to keep the animals safe.

Tell everyone how incredible it is to see these animals living free.

And share all the facts you have learned in this book with your friends!

Wacky Whale Facts

Harbor porpoises are known as "puffing pigs" because of the puffing sound they make as they breathe.

Sometimes, a male narwhal grows two tusks. Female narwhals may also grow a tusk, but this is very unusual.

A whale's tail is like your fingerprint. No two are the same!

Dolphins may join up to create a "superpod." There can be more than 1,000 dolphins hunting together.

A drone called SnotBot flies through a whale's spout and collects "snot" samples. The samples give scientists clues about the whale's health!

Hunting whales, dolphins, and porpoises is banned in most countries. But sadly, there are still some places around the world where people hunt these animals.

Snubfin dolphins like to spit water! Scientists think they do this to show off to their mates.
Snubfin dolphin
Dolphins have best friends! Male bottlenose dolphins team up to find food and stick up for each other.
Baby whales, dolphins, and porpoises are born tail first. The calf's head is born last, then mom guides her newborn straight to the water's surface to breathe.
Right whales are covered with bumpy patches called callosities. The patches look white because they are covered with thousands of tiny white lice!
Right whale bumpy patch

My Whale and Dolphin Words

baleen plates
Long, bristly parts that hang in the mouths of some types of whales. They trap tiny animals in the water.

blowhole
Nostril-like holes for breathing on the heads of whales, dolphins, and porpoises.

bonds
Ways in which animals help each other and feel close to each other.

breaching
Leaping from the water and splashing down again.

camouflage
Colors or patterns on an animal's body that help it blend into its background.

communicate
To share information and feelings by making sounds or using body language.

echolocation
Using clicking sounds and the echoes that bounce back to find prey.

extinct
Gone forever. For example, dinosaurs are extinct and gone forever.

flipper
A body part that is used by animals such as whales, dolphins, and seals for swimming.

fluke
The tail of a whale, dolphin, or porpoise.

fossil
The rocky remains of an animal or plant that lived millions of years ago.

mammal
An animal with hair or fur. Female mammals give birth to live babies and feed them milk.

mate
An animal's partner with which it has young. Also to come together to produce young.

migration
Moving from one place to another and then back again. For example, animals might migrate to find food.

plankton
Very tiny animals and plant-like living things that drift in oceans, lakes, rivers, and ponds.

predator
An animal that hunts and eats other animals.

prehistoric
A long, long time ago before people began recording history.

prey
An animal that is hunted by other animals for food.

skeleton
A framework of bones inside the body of an animal or person.

streamlined
Smooth with a shape that moves easily through water or air.

tracking device
A small device that's attached to an animal. It sends information to scientists—for example, where a whale travels.

warm-blooded
Able to make your own body heat , even if the air or water around you is cold. Mammals are warm-blooded.

zooplankton
Very tiny animals that drift in oceans, lakes, rivers, and ponds. Some are too small to see!

Big Whales and Dolphins Quiz

1: Which whale is the biggest?
- a) Humpback whale
- b) Gray whale
- c) Blue whale

2: What kind of animals are whales and dolphins?
- a) Fish
- b) Mammals
- c) Reptiles

3: What keeps whales and dolphins warm?
- a) Blubber
- b) The Sun
- c) Swimming fast

4: Which whale has a tusk?
- a) A beluga whale
- b) A narwhal
- c) An orca

5: How long can a bowhead whale live for?
- a) 200 years
- b) 20 years
- c) 2,000 years

6: What does baleen trap?
- a) Trash
- b) Sharks
- c) Plankton

7: What do dolphins use to find food?
- a) Breaching
- b) Echolocation
- c) Hydrophones

8: Who was a giant prehistoric whale?
- a) Whale-o-saurus
- b) Livyatan
- c) Megalodon

9: Which dolphin is the biggest?
- a) An orca
- b) A bottlenose dolphin
- c) A spinner dolphin

10: What type of journey do whales and dolphins go on?
- a) Vacation
- b) Migration
- c) Invitation

Answers:
1) c 2) b 3) a 4) b 5) a
6) c 7) b 8) b 9) a 10) b